I0420423

Foreword

The study of sociology has become very popular in the last two decades and learners have shown good response for the course study and opted this subject as one of the subjects in the competitive examinations as well. The subject has been introduced in the most of the higher education institutions in Jammu and Kashmir and good numbers of qualified people in the subject have been engaged as faculty. This response has motivated our young and talented faculty to write books on the subject. The book titled, "An Introduction to Sociology" by Dr. Fayaz Ahmad Bhat and Ajaz Ahmad Bhat, as co-authors is one of the examples. The book is based on the latest syllabus designed by the affiliated university and has very good getup. The endeavor of the authors shall be very useful to the student community in general and readers in particular. The writing of books is a need of an hour in the changed global scenario of ICT (Information Communication Technology) age. I congratulate the authors who have good aptitude towards teaching-learning process and wish them very bright future in the academics and personal life.

Prof. Fayaz Ahmad Mir
Principal
Govt. Degree College, Sumbal

Preface

Change is the law of nature. One who does not change with changing circumstances either perishes or remains backward mentally, physically, socially and educationally?

Education is the weapon that keeps an individual updated and helps him or her to change with the changing circumstances. Education system is not an exceptional. It is not exempted from the law of nature. No doubt education system is responsible for bringing changes in society however, it gets transformed with the changing surroundings and global environment.

The change in the pattern of education system has been a long pending demand of educationist, sociologists and social reformers. Finally, most of the higher educational institutions of the country have borrowed semester system from America at both under graduate and post graduate level.

By and large, semester system is perceived to be better than the annual system. The semester system keeps students busy throughout the year with academic endeavors and opens new horizons of learning. However, it is not a smooth walk for learners especially for student community. It unfolds new issues and challenges. Dedication, commitment and right track is the only strategy for success and maximum returns. The availability and selection of right, apprehensible and comprehensive material is one of the biggest challenges before the student community. The present book has been compiled by taking the issues and challenges of student community into due consideration. A number of reputed national and international books were flipped besides research papers and article to compose the book.

Authors

Dr. Fayaz Ahmad Bhat
And
Ajaz Ahmad Bhat

Contents

4.11	Secondary Group
4.12	Characteristics of Secondary Group
4.13	Importance of Secondary groups
4.14	Difference between Primary and Secondary group
4.15	Concept of Reference Group
4.16	Defining Reference Group
4.17	Characteristics of Reference Group
4.18	Importance of Reference Group
4.19	Difference between Primary and Reference Group
4.20	Concept of Role and Status
4.21	What is Role?
4.22	Types of Roles
4.23	Role Set
4.24	Characteristics of Role
4.25	Status
4.26	Types of Status
4.27	Explanation of Role and Status
4.28	Values
4.29	Norms
4.30	Characteristics of Norms

Chapter- I

1.01. Introduction: Sociology is one of the youngest sciences which originated in Europe about a hundred and fifty years ago. After World War Second the need for sociology was felt more and sociology developed very fast after the Second World War. This chapter defines sociology and discusses the nature scope and subject matter of sociology. This chapter traces the emergence of sociology and discusses factors responsible for the emergence of sociology.

1.02. What is Sociology? The term sociology is combination of two words *socius* and *logos*. The word *socius* is a Latin word meaning companion or associate and *logos* is a Greek word meaning study or science. Thus sociology means the science of society. Sociology studies society of group interaction and social behavior. Sociology uses scientific methods that are observation, experiments and comparison to study society. The world sociology was coined by August Comte in 1839 (Ritzer). August Comte is considered the founder of modern sociology thus called father of sociology.

There are many definitions of sociology given by various scholars. According to Curvier, J.F. sociology is "the method of discovery of the uniformities in the universe through the process of observation and re-observation…" Lundberg said that sociology is a "procedure" to discover the conditions under which things happen. According to Park sociology is the "the science of collective behavior".

Sociology is concerned with social relationships, relationships of an individual with other individuals. It study society as an interconnected altogether. Sociology is different from other social sciences as social relationship is main concern of sociology.

1.03. What is Science? Science is systematic knowledge that gained through observation, experiments and comparison.

1.04. Sociology as Science: Sociology is science of society. It studies society by using scientific methods that is observation, experiment and comparison. Sociology studies human beings in society, their behavior, relation and interaction with other human beings. The founding fathers of sociology Auguste Comte and Emile Durkhiem said that science of society is possible like the science of physics, chemistry, and biology. Auguste Comte said that we can know the history of human society with the help of sociology. Sociology can make us understand how society changed from one stage another.

1.05. Emergence of Sociology. Sociology emerged an independent subject and separate branch of knowledge in 19th century. It was social, political and economic changes in the Europe which brought sociology into existence. The sociological studies of human society first begin in Europe. There were many changes and development in 17th, 18th and 19th century in Europe which were responsible for the emergence of sociology. Industrial revolution, French revolution and Enlightenment movement were main factors responsible for the emergence of sociology. Auguste Comte, Emile Durkheim, Herbert Spencer and other thinkers played an important role.

1.06. Industrial Revolution. The Industrial revolution took place in Europe from 18th to 19th centuries. The revolution brought many changes in European society, new ways and means of manufacturing goods introduced in society. In this period large number of population in Europe and America shifted from agriculture and villages to industries and cities.

This brought major changes not in European and American society but also in other parts of the world.

The emergence of sociology is deeply associated with industrial revolution. Industrial revolution became one of the important reasons for the emergence of sociology. Industrial revolution brought basic changes in society and social relations. The means of communication, transportation, production and interactions were changed. There was change in family structure. The industrial revolution changed means of production, a large number of people shifted to industrial sector from agricultural sector. With the growth of industries in urban areas a large number of people migrated from rural areas to urban areas. This is called urbanization. The process of urbanization led many changes in both urban and rural areas. This also changed the character of old cities and towns. With this many new problems were introduced in urban and rural areas.

The growth and expansion of cities introduced new issues and problems. The main problems were over crowdedness, bad sanitation, pollution, deindustrialization, shortage in electricity, shortage of water, over crowed in public transport etc.

Industrial revolution also led the degradation of labour. There was exploitation of labour with no job security. The factory system destroyed peasants and artisan (NCERT,2006).

All the changes brought in by industrial revolution led many thinkers to think over the new social issues and problems scientifically. Many thinkers were concerned with these problems and issues and tried to find out solution to these problems. This led to emergence of sociology.

1.07. French Revolution: French revolution took place in France in 1789. The revolution brought basic changes in political, economic and social system. The revolution challenged traditional authority and abolished the monarchy. It ended feudalism and introduced new order. The revolution became turning point for freedom, equality, liberty, and democracy. The affects of revolution were not limited to France but had far reaching impact to whole globe. The ideas of liberty, democracy, equality, and fraternity were diffused globally. It generated idea of democracy all over the world and became foundation for emergence of new ideas.

French revolution brought many dramatic changes in French society. It changed class structure, political set up and economy. Aristocrats who enjoyed power and prestige lost their status and money. Peasants who were at the bottom of society and had low status gained power. They occupied influential positions in society. This brought new changes and challenges in the society. The old system of society based on tradition, religion, kinship, land and class was challenged. New ideologies of socialism, democracy, equality and individualism have birth.

Many thinkers of that time were concerned with the new social and political set up. They were concerned with the problems of society and tried to find solution to them. According to Berger and Berger, French revolution introduced both positive and negative changes in society. It was the negative changes which became reason for the emergence of sociology.

According to Nisbert, it is a fact that French revolution was responsible for the emergence of sociology. It has great role in the development of sociological concepts and theories. August Comte the father of sociology had great influence of French revolution. The events which took place during

French revolution became bases for August Comte and sociology.

1.08. Enlightenment Period: Enlighten simply means to make clear, to understand and to clear confusion. Enlightenment movement took place in Europe from about 17th until 18th centuries. Enlightenment is known as age of reason and logic in which people started to think on the bases of reason and logic. Importance was given to reason and individualism. Science advanced greatly in this period. The traditional way of thinking and explanation of things was challenged in this period. The authority of social institutions like Church was challenged. Social reform movements were launched and science was given importance. Science and scientific development

The emergence of sociology as a science of society is greatly related to Enlightenment period. In this period basic changes were experienced in Europe. Traditional thinking was replaced by modern thinking. It introduced new thinking, new concepts and new way of looking at things. Critical and constructive thinking was introduced in society in the Enlightenment period.

Darwin and his theory of evolution were influential in developing new concepts and thinking. Enlightenment period makes some people believe that society can be studied by using scientific methods that is observation, experiment and comparison. It was believed that human beings are rational and they can understand social relation and human behavior rationally. The new thinking introduced by enlightenment movement was responsible for industrial revolution and scientific revolution which ultimately led the emergence of sociology.

1.09. Nature of Sociology: Nature simply means essential qualities or characteristics of something. Every subject has its essential qualities and characteristics similarly sociology has its own essential qualities. Sociology as a branch of knowledge has its own and different qualities and characteristics. It is social science but different from other social science. Sociology has its own subject matter that is human society and their relations. It is science of society. Rao (1990) said that Biertedt has given many characteristics of sociology some of them are as follows:

i. Sociology is an independent Science: According to Robert Biertedt sociology is scientific study of society. It studies society independently as it is not branch of any subject.

ii. Sociology is social science: Like political science, economics, psychology, philosophy, history and anthropology sociology is social science not a physical science. Sociology study human beings in society their behavior, and relations. It studies human organisation and functioning of social groups.

iii. Sociology is a categorical nor a normative discipline: By categorical we mean that sociology is an unconditional science it is not influenced by values and norms. Sociology does not say how society, social life should be but it says what and how things are. It does not judge what is good or bad, just and unjust, moral and immoral. Sociology is an objective science.

iv. Sociology is pure science not Applied science: By pure science we do not mean that sociology is physical science like physics, chemistry and biology but like pure sciences make task of sociology is to acquire knowledge. Sociologists are not concerned whether their knowledge will be applied or appreciated. Sociological knowledge may or may not be used a sociologist is least concerned with it.

v. **Sociology is a general science not a special social science**: Unlike other social science- economics, political science, history sociology does not study human beings independent of other social institutions; it studies social life in general. Sociology does not focus only on any particular aspect in society it studies social life in general.

vi. Sociology is both Rational and Empirical: The sociological knowledge is not based on myth, guess or intuition but based and supported by science. It uses both rationalism and empiricism.

Besides above mentioned characteristics the main characteristics of sociology are that it defines a problem which it studies.

It collects data systematically on the defined problem

It formulates hypothesis

It analysis the collected data

It tests the hypothesis

It interprets the collected data

And finally it draws conclusion.

1. 10. Subject Matter of Sociology: Not only subject matter of physical sciences and social sciences is different but it is different to every subject. Physics, chemistry, sociology economics all have a different subject matter. The founding father of sociology August Comte has divide sociology into Social Dynamics and Social Statics. The study of social order is Social Statics and the study social change and progress is Social Dynamics. Thus according August Comte both social order and social change is subject matter of sociology.

Sociologists have agreed that following is the subject matter of sociology:

Sociology is concerned with human society, their behavior and interaction. It studies family, marriage, kinship, social institutions, and social processes.

Sociology studies society from sociological perspective.

Sociology studies both order and change in society. It studies how social institutions are playing their role. It also studies how there has been change in social institutions. What stages a society has gone through and how society has progressed from one stage to another.

Sociology studies also the function and dysfunction of things in society. It observes what function a particular social institution is performing in the function of society.

Sociology attempts to be more rational and empirical. It focuses on scientific means and methods in analysis of society.

1.11. Long Answer Type Questions

Q. How industrial Revolution, French Revolution and Enlightenment Movement led to the Rise of Sociology.

Or

Q. What were factors responsible for the emergence of Sociology? Discuss

Or

Q. What were the factors responsible for the origin and development of Sociology? Discuss

Or

Q. Write a note on the history of sociology.

Ans. Sociology is youngest social science. Sociology emerged in Europe. It emerged and developed in a particular social, political and economic background. There were many changes in Europe Industrial revolution, French Revolution became main factors for the emergence of sociology.

Industrial revolution: The Industrial revolution took place in Europe from 18th to 19th centuries. The revolution brought many changes in European society, new ways and means of manufacturing goods introduced in society. In this period large number of population in Europe and America shifted from agriculture and villages to industries and cities. This brought major changes not in European and American society but also in other parts of the world.

The emergence of sociology is deeply associated with industrial revolution. Industrial revolution became one of the important reasons for the emergence of sociology. Industrial revolution brought basic changes in society and social relations. The means of communication, transportation, production and interactions were changed. There was change in family structure. The industrial revolution changed means of production, a large number of people shifted to industrial sector from agricultural sector. With the growth of industries in urban areas a large number of people migrated from rural areas to urban areas. This is called urbanization. The process of urbanization led many changes in both urban and rural areas. This also changed the character of old cities and towns. With this many new problems were introduced in urban and rural areas.

The growth and expansion of cities introduced new issues and problems. The main problems were over crowdedness, bad sanitation, pollution, deindustrialization, shortage in electricity, shortage of water, over crowed in public transport etc.

Industrial revolution also led the degradation of labour. There was exploitation of labour with no job security. The factory system destroyed peasants and artisan

All the changes brought in by industrial revolution led many thinkers to think over the new social issues and problems scientifically. Many thinkers were concerned with these problems and issues and tried to find out solution to these problems. This led to emergence of sociology.

French Revolution: French revolution took place in France in 1789. The revolution brought basic changes in political, economic and social system. The revolution challenged traditional authority and abolished the monarchy. It ended feudalism in Europe and introduced new social order. The revolution became turning point for freedom, equality, liberty, and democracy. The affects of revolution were not limited to France but had far reaching impact to whole globe. The ideas of liberty, democracy, equality, and fraternity were diffused globally. It generated idea of democracy all over the world and became foundation for emergence of new ideas.

French revolution brought many dramatic changes in French society. It changed class structure, political set up and economy. Aristocrats who enjoyed power and prestige lost their status and money. Peasants who were at the bottom of society and had low status gained power. They occupied influential positions in society. This brought new changes and challenges in the society. The old system of society based on tradition, religion, kinship, land and class was challenged. New ideologies of socialism, democracy, equality and individualism have birth.

Many thinkers of that time were concerned with the new social and political set up. They were concerned with the problems of society and tried to find solution to them. According to Berger and Berger, French revolution introduced both positive and negative changes in society. It was the negative changes which became reason for the emergence of sociology.

According to Nisbert, it is a fact that French revolution was responsible for the emergence of sociology. It has great role in the development of sociological concepts and theories. August Comte the father of sociology had great influence of French revolution. The events which took place during French revolution became bases for August Comte and sociology.

Enlightenment Movement: Enlightenment movement took place in Europe from about 17th until 18th centuries. Enlightenment is known as age of reason and logic in which people started to think on the bases of reason and logic. Importance was given to reason and individualism. Science advanced greatly in this period. The traditional way of thinking and explanation of things was challenged in this period. The authority of social institutions like Church was challenged. Social reform movements were launched and science was given importance. Science and scientific development

The emergence of sociology as a science of society is greatly related to Enlightenment period. In this period basic changes were experienced in Europe. Traditional thinking was replaced by modern thinking. It introduced new thinking, new concepts and new way of looking at things. Critical and constructive thinking was introduced in society in the Enlightenment period.

Darwin and his theory of evolution were influential in developing new concepts and thinking. Enlightenment period makes some people believe that society can be studied by using scientific methods that is observation, experiment and comparison. It was believed that human beings are rational and they can understand social relation and human behavior rationally. The new thinking introduced by enlightenment movement was responsible for industrial revolution and scientific revolution which ultimately led the emergence of sociology.

Q. Write a detailed note on the nature of sociology.

OR

What is Nature of Sociology? Explain

Ans. Nature of Sociology: Nature simply means essential qualities or characteristics of something. Every subject has its essential qualities and characteristics similarly sociology has its own essential qualities. Sociology as a branch of knowledge has its own and different qualities and characteristics. It is social science but different from other social science. Sociology has its own subject matter that is human society and their relations. It is science of society. Biertedt has given many characteristics of sociology some of them are as follows:

1. Sociology is an independent Science: According to Robert Biertedt sociology is scientific study of society. It studies society independently as it is not branch of any subject.

2. Sociology is social science: Like political science, economics, psychology, philosophy, history and anthropology sociology is social science not a physical science. Sociology study human beings in society their behavior, and relations. It studies human organisation and functioning of social groups.

3. **Sociology is a categorical nor a normative discipline:** By categorical we mean that sociology is an unconditional science it is not influenced by values and norms. Sociology does not say how society, social life should be but it says what and how things are. It does not judge what is good or bad, just and unjust, moral and immoral. Sociology is an objective science.

4.Sociology is pure science not Applied science: By pure science we do not mean that sociology is physical science like physics, chemistry and biology but like pure sciences make task of sociology is to acquire knowledge. Sociologists are not concerned whether their knowledge will be applied or appreciated. Sociological knowledge may or may not be used a sociologist is least concerned with it.

5. Sociology is a general science not a special social science: Unlike other social science- economics, political science, history sociology does not study human beings independent of other social institutions; it studies social life in general. Sociology does not focus only on any particular aspect in society it studies social life in general.

6. Sociology is both Rational and Empirical: The sociological knowledge is not based on myth, guess or intuition but based and supported by science. It uses both rationalism and empiricism.

Besides above mentioned characteristics the main characteristics of sociology are that it defines a problem which it studies.

It collects data systematically on the defined problem

It formulates hypothesis

It analysis the collected data

It tests the hypothesis

It interprets the collected data

And finally it draws conclusion.

Q. Write a detailed note on Sociology. How sociology is a science

Or

What is Sociology? How Sociology is a science.

Or

Sociology is science of society. Explain

Ans. The term sociology is combination of two words *socius* and *logos*. The word *socius* is a Latin word meaning companion or associate and *logos* is a Greek word meaning study or science. Thus sociology means the science of society. Sociology studies society of group interaction and social behavior. Sociology uses scientific methods that are observation, experiments and comparison to study society. The world sociology was coined by August Comte in 1839. August Comte is considered the founder of modern sociology thus called father of sociology.

There are many definitions of sociology given by various scholars. According to Curvier, J.F. sociology is "the method of discovery of the uniformities in the universe through the process of observation and re-observation…" Lundberg said that sociology is a "procedure" to discover the conditions under which things happen. According to Park sociology is the "the science of collective behavior".

Sociology is concerned with social relationships, relationships of an individual with other individuals. It study society as an interconnected altogether. Sociology is different from other social sciences as social relationship is main concern of sociology.

Sociology as Science: Sociology is science of society. It studies society by using scientific methods that is observation, experiment and comparison. Sociology studies human beings in society, their behavior, relation and interaction with other human beings. The founding fathers of sociology Auguste Comte and Emile Durkhiem said that science of society is possible like the science of physics, chemistry, and biology. Auguste Comte said that we can know the history of human society with the help of sociology. Sociology can make us understand how society changed from one stage another.

1.12. Short Answer Type Questions

Q. Define Sociology

Or

What is sociology?

Ans. Sociology is a social science. It studies man and his relations in society scientifically.The term sociology are combination of two words *socius* and *logos*. The word *socius* is a Latin word meaning companion or associate and *logos* is a Greek word meaning study or science. Thus sociology means the science of society. Sociology studies society of group interaction and social behavior. Sociology uses scientific methods that are observation, experiments and comparison to study society. The world sociology was coined by August Comte in 1839. August Comte is considered the founder of modern sociology thus called father of sociology.

There are many definitions of sociology given by various scholars. According to Curvier, J.F. sociology is "the method of discovery of the uniformities in the universe through the process of observation and re-observation..."

Q. What is Subject Matter of Sociology?

Or

Q. Discuss Subject Matter of Sociology

Ans. Subject Matter of Sociology: Sociology is an independent science. It has its own subject matter. Not only the subject matter of physical sciences and social sciences are different but it is different to social sciences. Physics, chemistry, sociology economics all have a different subject matter. The founding father of sociology August Comte has divide sociology into Social Dynamics and Social Statics. The study of social order is Social Statics and the study social change and progress is Social Dynamics. Thus according August Comte both social order and social change is subject matter of sociology.

Sociologists have agreed that following is the subject matter of sociology:

Sociology is concerned with human society, their behavior and interaction. It studies family, marriage, kinship, social institutions, and social processes.

Sociology studies society from sociological perspective.

Sociology studies both order and change in society. It studies how social institutions are playing their role. It also studies how there has been change in social institutions. What stages a society has gone through and how society has progressed from one stage to another.

Sociology studies also the function and dysfunction of things in society. It observes what function a particular social institution is performing in the function of society.

Sociology attempts to be more rational and empirical. It focuses on scientific means and methods in analysis of society.

<u>Chapter-II</u>

2.01. Introduction: This is the second chapter of the book. This chapter will demonstrate relation of sociology with other social sciences- Anthropology, Economics, History, Political Science, Philosophy and Psychology.

2.02. Relation Sociology with other Social Sciences: Sociology is not only social science. Political science, Economics, Psychology, History, Anthropology, Philosophy are other important social science. Every subject contributes in the field of knowledge and study social universe. They (social sciences) study different aspects of human society: social, political, economical, historical, cultural, psychological and environmental. However, the boundaries and subject matter of every subjected is confined and limited. Many times they study different facets of same social reality (Rao,1990). Social sciences are not poles apart from each other. They are interdependent and interdisciplinary borrow concepts, theories methods and techniques from each other and help each other in better understanding of social reality. There is constant give and take process among various social sciences. The advancement in one subject influences the study in another and opens different dimensions of social reality.

Sociology does not claim an all inclusive science of society which absorbs other social science. Sociology is the youngest of all social science which emerged as separate and independent in the backdrop of industrial revolution, French revolution and Enlightenment in Nineteenth century. The boundaries of sociology are wider in comparison to other social sciences. Sociology is scientific study of human society and human relations and society is common base of all social sciences.

2.03. Relation of Sociology with Anthropology

The relationship between sociology and anthropology is so close that many people find it difficult to make difference between the two (sociology and anthropology). Kroeber said that two subjects are twin sisters. It becomes difficult for many to demarcate the boundaries of two disciplines as area of study of the two disciplines overlap. Both the disciplines are social science and share many concepts and theories. Ethnographic methods used by anthropology are also used by sociology and many sociological studies are using the method. Natural science especially biology nourished both sociology and anthropology.

Despite much similarity between sociology and anthropology there is a lot of difference between the two disciplines. Sociology and anthropology have also different sources of origin. Sociology which is a youngest science originated out of philosophy and European tradition of social and political philosophy. Anthropology developed out of physical anthropology and nourished by biology (Kar, 1979).

Anthropology literally means the study of man. The word anthropology has been derived from the Greek words – *Anthropos* meaning man and *logos* meaning study. There are many branches of anthropology like archaeology, linguistics, physical anthropology, and social anthropology. The physical anthropology studies physical aspects of humans classified in various groups. Social anthropology studies culture and social life of human beings. It was earlier argued that anthropology studies culture of early or primitive societies and sociology studies modern or present society. This argument and distinction is no longer accepted.

Anthropology studies humans and their culture. It provides sociology important data related to culture. Sociology studies social groups; their culture, organisation, behavior and institutions. Sociology has been greatly benefited by anthropology. Linton and Brown Makinowski have greatly explored the advantage (Kachroo and Kachroo1999). A number of village studies in India have been done by social anthropologist besides a large number of tribal societies. Anthropology helps sociologist in better understanding social phenomenon and social institutions. The origin of society, marriage and private property are better understood by using anthropological data.

The scope of anthropology is wide while as scope of sociology is narrow in comparison to anthropology.

2.04. Relation of Sociology with Economics

Sociology and economics have close relation with each other and are connected mutually. The relation between the two is so close that economic is treated as a branch of sociology. According to Thomas "Economics is, in fact, but one branch of the comprehensive science of sociology..." Both sociology and economics are social sciences concerned with social universe. Knowledge is common aim of both the disciplines and society is common base for them. They borrow concepts, theories, and methods from each other and influence studies each other. Many economists were also sociologist and contributed in the field of both sociology and economics. Karl Marx , Max Weber, C.H Cooly, Bowels, Gintis are few examples. Parson said that economic behavior of a society cannot be understood in isolation of social milieu. In the recent past interaction between two subjects have increased. For example many sociological studies have directly studied problems of economic theory, Barbara Cotton's book "The Social Foundation of Wage Policy" is a recent example.

Economics is mainly concerned with production, distribution of goods and services. It studies economic activities and behavior of society. The classical economics studied interrelationship between price, demand and supply of goods. The focus of economics was earlier very narrow. Economics studies mainly interrelation of economic factors: the relation between price and supply, demand and supply, money flow and input-output ratios. Economy makes the main problem of economics. Economics and sociology certain times study same thing but study them differently for example both study industry but study differently. Economics study labour, production, marketing etc., where as sociology study the impact of industry or industrialization on society.

The scope and boundaries of economics are confined and limited while as scope and boundaries of sociology are wider. Sociology studies all kinds of social relations and takes into consideration the influence of other social factors like belief, religion and culture on economic activities of society. Economics on the other hand studies only those factors which are economic in nature. Sociology is promotes critical thinking and tries to look hidden factors of social problem. It gives clear understanding of social situations of past and present. It uses both qualitative and quantitative methods in understanding social reality. In sum up it can be concluded that the boundaries of sociology are wider than economics. However, that does not mean that economics has no role and place.

2.05. Relation of Sociology with History

Sociology and history are very much interconnected with each other. Both are social sciences and inter- disciplinary. Many concepts and theories used by history are used by sociology. A number of historians have also been sociologists Karl Marx, is an example. History is the story of early human societies. It narrates their emergence, survival, social set up, belief system and culture. According to Howard, "history is past of sociology and sociology is present history".

History study the past while as sociology studies contemporary society or recent past societies. History excludes nothing. Anything that takes place is subject matter of history. The subject matter of conventional history has been about the past of kings and wars. Historians earlier were trying to define the actual issues, to demonstrate how things actually took place, while as sociology tries to know casual relationships.

History gives sociology data. It helps sociology in understanding social reality as it gives sociology context of things. History studies concrete details of events while as sociology more likely studies abstract from concrete reality. There is no doubt that history have great influence on sociology however, sociology too has influenced history. With the influence of sociology over history, history has become sociological. Early historical studies were not focusing on sociological aspects of things like gender, family etc which is not a case now. History now also focuses upon customs, values, beliefs and gender relations.

Everything which happens in sociology is concern of history but all history is not sociological. It studies concrete details.

2.06. Relation of Sociology with Political Science

Sociology and political science are closely interrelated and connected mutually. Both have close relation with each other and borrow concepts, theories and research techniques from each other. Sometimes it is difficult to demarcate the boundaries of political science and sociology. Sociology emerged an independent branch of knowledge in the backdrop of political conditions of Europe and French revolution was one of the main factors responsible for the emergence of sociology. According to Morris Ginsberg, "historically, sociology has its roots in politics and philosophy of history". Both Sociology and political science have profound impact on each other and have separate branch which are concerned with political aspects and social aspects. There is separate branch of study in sociology known as political sociology which is exclusively concerned with political behavior of human society. In political science sociological theories and concepts are used to have a better understanding of a political system of a country. Political activities of a person are influenced by social factors and social activities of a person are affected by political factors.

Political science is mainly concerned with the study of state and its elements. The main focus of traditional political science was on political theory and government administration. Sociology however studies every aspect of society. It studies relationship between various institutions including government, economic and religious.

Many sociologists and political scientists were also political scientists philosophers both political scientists

2.07. Relation between Sociology and Philosophy

The relation between sociology and philosophy are very close to each other. Sociology has emerged an independent science of society in 19th century it was earlier a branch of philosophy. Sociology was earlier known as mental philosophy, or the philosophy of mind. There is still a lot of bearing of philosophy on sociology and it would not be wrong to say that sociology without philosophy is impossible. Sociology has to keep itself side by side of the philosophical basis. A sociologist cannot understand social reality unless he/she is familiar with the philosophical basis of society he/she is studying. Only by some training in social philosophy can a sociologist understand and explain a social phenomenon, (Kar,1964).

The word philosophy has been derived from Greek ..... which means 'love of wisdom'? Philosophy is concerned with getting knowledge regarding causes and laws of everything.

2.08. Relation of Sociology with Psychology: There is controversy among sociologist relating to relation of sociology and psychology. Durkheim believed that sociology should study only *social facts* not psychological factors while as Mill, Ginsberg and Max Weber have different opinion. Weber believed that sociological studies can be more enriched with the help of psychology. Despite controversy on the issue both the subjects are interdependent on each other and have close relation with each other. Both the subjects are social sciences and interdependent on each other. Psychological development is highly dependent on social interaction psychological factors are important for social structure. Understanding the psychology of an individual is very difficult to understand without understanding his/her social background. To have better understanding of social institutions and their growth it is important to understand the psychology of humans.

The two subject share concepts, theories and methods with each other. Many sociological theories are used by psychologists to understand their subject matter and many psychological theories are used by sociologist to understand social reality. Many sociologists a have contributed in psychology and many psychologists have also contributed in sociology C. H. Cooly, Mead, Summner are few examples. Despite interdependence of the two on each other there is controversy on the relation of two.

Psychology is science of human of behavior. It studies the human mind thus concerned with mental system. The man focus of psychology is an individual. It studies intelligence, memory, motivation and learning of an individual. Sociology is the study of social system. It studies social process like cooperation, conflict, completion accommodation and acculturation.

2.09. Long Answer type Questions

Q. What is Relationship between Economics and Sociology?

Ans. Sociology and economics have close relation with each other and are connected mutually. The relation between the two is so close that economic is treated as a branch of sociology. According to Thomas "Economics is, in fact, but one branch of the comprehensive science of sociology…" Both sociology and economics are social sciences concerned with social universe. Knowledge is common aim of both the disciplines and society is common base for them. They borrow concepts, theories, and methods from each other and influence studies each other. Many economists were also sociologist and contributed in the field of both sociology and economics. Karl Marx , Max Weber, C.H Cooly, Bowels, Gintis are few examples. Parson said that economic behavior of a society cannot be understood in isolation of social milieu. In the recent past interaction between two subjects have increased. For example many sociological studies have directly studied problems of economic theory, Barbara Cotton's book "The Social Foundation of Wage Policy" is a recent example.

Economics is mainly concerned with production, distribution of goods and services. It studies economic activities and behavior of society. The classical economics studied interrelationship between price, demand and supply of goods. The focus of economics was earlier very narrow. Economics studies mainly interrelation of economic factors: the relation between price and supply, demand and supply, money flow and input-output ratios. Economy makes the main problem of economics. Economics and sociology certain times study same thing but study them differently for example both study industry but study differently. Economics study labour, production, marketing etc., where as sociology study the impact of industry or industrialization on society.

The scope and boundaries of economics are confined and limited while as scope and boundaries of sociology are wider. Sociology studies all kinds of social relations and takes into consideration the influence of other social factors like belief, religion and culture on economic activities of society. Economics on the other hand studies only those factors which are economic in nature. Sociology is promotes critical thinking and tries to look hidden factors of social problem. It gives clear understanding of social situations of past and present. It uses both qualitative and quantitative methods in understanding social reality. In sum up it can be concluded that the boundaries of sociology are wider than economics. However, that does not mean that economics has no role and place.

Q. What is relation between Sociology and Psychology?

Ans. There is controversy among sociologist relating to relation of sociology and psychology. Durkheim believed that sociology should study only *social facts* not psychological factors while as Mill, Ginsberg and Max Weber have different opinion. Weber believed that sociological studies can be more enriched with the help of psychology. Despite controversy on the issue both the subjects are interdependent on each other and have close relation with each other. Both the subjects are social sciences and interdependent on each other. Psychological development is highly dependent on social interaction psychological factors are important for social structure. Understanding the psychology of an individual is very difficult to understand without understanding his/her social background. To have better understanding of social institutions and their growth it is important to understand the psychology of humans.

 The two subject share concepts, theories and methods with each other. Many sociological theories are used by psychologists to understand their subject matter and many psychological theories are used by sociologist to understand social reality. Many sociologists a have contributed in psychology and many psychologists have also contributed in sociology C. H. Cooly, Mead, Summner are few examples. Despite interdependence of the two on each other there is controversy on the relation of two.

Psychology is science of human of behavior. It studies the human mind thus concerned with mental system. The man focus of psychology is an individual. It studies intelligence, memory, motivation and learning of an individual. Sociology is the study of social system. It studies social process like cooperation, conflict, completion accommodation and acculturation.

Q. Discuss Relationship between Sociology and History.

Ans. Sociology and history are very much interconnected with each other. Both are social sciences and inter-disciplinary. Many concepts and theories used by history are used by sociology. A number of historians have also been sociologists Karl Marx, is an example. History is the story of early human societies. It narrates their emergence, survival, social set up, belief system and culture. According to Howard, "history is past of sociology and sociology is present history".

History study the past while as sociology studies contemporary society or recent past societies. History excludes nothing. Anything that takes place is subject matter of history. The subject matter of conventional history has been about the past of kings and wars. Historians earlier were trying to define the actual issues, to demonstrate how things actually took place, while as sociology tries to know casual relationships.

History gives sociology data. It helps sociology in understanding social reality as it gives sociology context of things. History studies concrete details of events while as sociology more likely studies abstract from concrete reality. There is no doubt that history have great influence on sociology however, sociology too has influenced history. With the influence of sociology over history, history has become sociological. Early historical studies were not focusing on sociological aspects of things like gender, family etc which is not a case now. History now also focuses upon customs, values, beliefs and gender relations.

Everything which happens in sociology is concern of history but all history is not sociological. It studies concrete details

2.10. Short Answer Type Questions

Q. Write a short note on relation of sociology with other social sciences.

Ans. Sociology is not only social science. Political science, Economics, Psychology, History, Anthropology, Philosophy are other important social science. Every subject contributes in the field of knowledge and study social universe. They study different aspects of human society: social, political, economical, historical, cultural, psychological and environmental. However, the boundaries and subject matter of every subjected is confined and limited. Many times they study different facets of same social reality. Social sciences are not poles apart from each other. They are interdependent and interdisciplinary borrow concepts, theories methods and techniques from each other and help each other in better understanding of social reality. There is constant give and take process among various social sciences. The advancement in one subject influences the study in another and opens different dimensions of social reality.

Q. What is relation of Sociology with Philosophy?

Ans. The relation between sociology and philosophy are very close to each other. Sociology has emerged an independent science of society in 19th century it was earlier a branch of philosophy. Sociology was earlier known as mental philosophy, or the philosophy of mind. There is still a lot of bearing of philosophy on sociology and it would not be wrong to say that sociology without philosophy is impossible. Sociology has to keep itself side by side of the philosophical basis. A sociologist cannot understand social reality unless he/she is familiar with the philosophical basis of society he/she is studying. Only by some training in social philosophy can a sociologist understand and explain a social phenomenon.

Chapter- III

3.01. Introduction. The very existence and foundation of sociology is based on society. Sociology is nothing but science of society. Without society there would have been no sociology. The concept of society is very fundamental in sociology. This chapter defines concept and characteristics of society. Various definitions given by sociologist about society are presented in the chapter.

3. 02. Concept of Society: The word society has been derived from the Latin word *'socius'* which means companion or associate. Society has been defined differently by various sociologists. There is not a single definition of society which is accepted by all sociologists. Sociologist is viewed as web of relationships. In this web an individual is related to other fellow being with different relations, relation of a teacher, student, buyer or seller etc. Society is not important for any particular individual but mandatory for every human. Men and women cannot live without society. Society is very fundamental for human beings. Human beings are just biological beings when they are born. They are made social beings by society. Aristotle very rightly said that "man is a social animal", he or she cannot live without society. Whether human beings live in rich or poor countries, villages or cities they live in society.

3.03. Meaning of Society: Society is a collection of people who live together and are bound in social relationship. In a relationship which is decided by mutual awareness of people who live together.

Society is not a material concept. It is an abstract concept, "which becomes institutionalized when people are related to one another in well-established and familiar ways" (ESO-11). Sociologists say that society exists only when people know each other and possess common interests (Bhushan and Sachdeva, 2013).

3.04. Types of Society: Sociologists have divided societies into various types. They divided societies on the bases of size and economy. Emile Durkheim and Herbert Spencer divided societies on the basis of their size and other features such as division of labour, political organisation etc. Karl Marx divided societies on the basis of their economic activities. Societies have been broadly divided into two types, simple and complex societies. All primitive societies are included in simple societies. The modern industrial societies are included among complex societies.

3.05. Defining Society: There is no single universally accepted definition of society. Different sociologists have defined society differently. Some of the definitions give by sociologist are as follows:

i. According to MacIver and Page, "Society is a system of usages and procedures, authority and mutual aid, of many groupings and divisions of controls of human behavior and liberties.

ii. "Society is complex of organized associations and institutions with a community", said, G.D.M. Cole

iii. MacIver, said society is "a web of social relationships"

iv. "Society includes not only the political relations by which men are bound together but whole range of human relations and collective activities". Leacock said.

v. According to Green, "A society is the larger group to which any individual belongs".

vi. Giddings, defined sociology as "the union itself, the organisation, the sum of formal relations in which associating individuals are bound together."

vii.Ginseberg, said that "A society is collection of individuals united by certain relations or modes of behavior which mark them off from others who do not enter into these relations or who differ from them in behavior".

viii. According to Lapiere, "The term society refers not to group of people, but to the complex pattern of the norms of interaction, that arise among between them.

ix. Parsons said "Society may be defined as the total complex of human relationships in so far as they grow out of action in terms of mean-end relationship, intrinsic or symbolic".

x. "Society is not a group of people; it is the system of relationships that exists between the individuals of the group." *Wright,* defined.

xi. According to Cooley, "Society is a complex of forms or processes each of which is living and growing by interaction with others, the whole being so unified that what takes place in one part affects all the rest."

3.06. Features /Elements or Characteristics of society:
There are various features of a society; some of them are as follows:

i. Collection of Humans: The first and the foremost important feature of society is that it is collection of individuals. As there can be no life without water and oxygen on the earth similarly there can no society without humans on the earth.

ii. Interdependence: Human beings are interdependent on each other for sustenance. Interdependence is another important feature of human society.

iii. Interaction: Whatever may be the type of a society- simple or complex, members of a society continuously interact with each other.

iv. Mutual Awareness: The mere collection of individuals does not constitute society. The members of society must be mutually aware of their relationship; the behavior of one person influences the behavior of other. According to Bhushan and Sachdeva, the journey of two persons in a train in a same compartment does not make them society. But their mutual awareness make the so.

v. Likeness: One of the important features of all societies is likeness. No matter whether it is rural or urban society, modern or traditional society likeness among members is very essential. According to MacIver "society means likeness". People in society have likeness with respect to their daily, needs, norms and values.

vii. Differences: In addition to likeness, difference is another essential feature of a society. Differences are not found only in modern societies but in simple and tribal societies also. I simple and tribal society people have differences based on age and sex and in modern societies it is based on wealth, power, occupation and education.

viii. Cooperation: Cooperation is one of the most important features of a society. Cooperation is the fundamental feature needed by a society; a society cannot exist without cooperation.

ix. Division of labour: Division of labour in society means assignment different jobs to different members of society. The assignment of these jobs is decided by culture, norm and values of society. The cooperation in a society is mostly possible with the division of labour. The division of labour in society keeps members interdependent.

x. Social Control: Social control is one of the important features of a society. To check the behavior of members and make them to follow norms and values of society social control is used. The behavior of members of society is regulated through social control. It protects from becoming deviant or rebellious. Social control is also used to suppress rebellion, revolt and conflict in society.

xi. Dynamic: Change is the law of Nature. Society is dynamic, no society ever remains same, and every society changes with changing times. Old members of a society die and new ones are born. There is change in social institution and norms of a society.

3.07. Concept of Community: Human beings live in society. They can't live without society. In one way or other they are in relation with other fellow beings. These relations vary to persons to persons with some fellow beings he she have intimate or close relations. He/she is related to other fellow beings as neighbor, villager, urban etc. The relation and intimacy is decided by his/ her background, two persons living in a same neighborhood have close relations than two persons living in a same village. Similarly two persons belonging to a same district have less close interaction and relations than two persons living in a same village.

People living in a definite territory have a sense of belongingness or sense of feeling. The kind of sense and belonging is basis for community.

Defining Community: The word community has been derived from old French word *comunete* means commonness or everybody. The word has also its origin in Latin word *communis* meaning common or fellowship.

Community is an organisation of human beings who have some sense of we-feeling and belongingness. Community is a group of people living in a definite area or territory and has common sentiments or feelings.

According to MacIver, locality and community sentiments are the bases of community.

1. Locality: Locality simply means physical basis of community (Rao, 2008). A group of people do not make a community unless they live in a territorial area. When people live together the interaction between them is personal. They develop close relations with each other and they develop a sense of belongingness.

ii. Community Sentiments: The second important thing for a group of people to form community is community sentiments. Locality alone is not sufficient for a group of people to form community. Besides occupying a territorial area community sentiments are important.

Community sentiments mean that members of a community have sense of belongingness. The members of a community must feel that they belong to a particular group and area. The members of a community must share some common interests. Sharing common interests are not enough to form a community, locality that is a definite territory is mandatory.

3.08. Sociological Definitions of Community: According of Kingsley Davis defined community a "smallest territorial group that can embrace all aspects of social life"

MacIver said community "is the term we apply to a pioneer settlement, a village, a city, a tribe, or a nation. Wherever the members of any group, small or large, live together in such a way that they share, not this or that particular interest, but the basic conditions of a common life, we call that group a community".

For Manheim " any circle of people who live together and belong together in such a way that they do not share this or that particular interest only, but a whole set of interests".

According to Ginsberg community is "a group of social beings living a common life including all the infinite variety and complexity of relations which result from that common life which constitutes it".

Parsons said "a community is that collectivity the members of which share a common territorial area as their base of operation for daily activities".

For Bogardus, "community is a social group with some degree of 'we feeling' and 'living in a given area'".

3.09. Characteristics and features of Community:

Community is a group of people having locality and we-feeling. Following are the main characteristics of community.

i. Group of People: The very foundation of community is human beings. There certain species who live in society and communities but sociology is not concerned with them sociology is concerned with human community.

ii. Locality: Locality means that people live together in a particular geographical area. Locality gives strong social bond between members of society. The physical boundaries of a community are clearly demarcated. The members of a community make change their locality from time to time as done by tribes and nomads.

iii. Close social relations: When people live in a definite territory they develop close relation with each other. In a community members have close relation with each other.

iv. We-feeling: People living in a community have always feeling of belongingness. The members have common interests and we feeling.

v. Cultural Similarity: the members of a community have mostly common belief system, norms and values. Their food habits and other activities are almost similar. They have culture similarity.

vi. Natural: Communities are not formed by individuals on their choice but are natural. An individual is not born in a community according to his/her wish.

vii. Permanent: Community is not something which can be abolished. Community is permanent.

viii. Likeness: Likeness dominates a community. The members of a community are like in respect of language, customs, and norm.

ix. Particular Name: Every community is known by a particular name.

3.10. Difference and Relation between Community and Society.

Society and community are two important concepts in sociology. The two concepts are many times confused with each other and used as synonyms. Despite community and society have close relation with each other there are certain differences between the two? Following table highlights main relations and differences between community and society.

S. No	Community	Society
1.	Community is an element of society	There are many communities within a society.
2.	A definite territory is important for community	A definite territory for society is not necessary.
3.	The size of community is small	There is no limit in the size of community.
4.	Members of a community have sense of we- feeling and belongingness	They may not be sense of we - feeling and belongingness in a society.
6.	Members of a community live in a common area	Members of a society do not live in a common area
7.	Members of a community have cultural similarity	Members of a society may not have cultural similarity
8.	Community sentiments are must for community	Community sentiments are not important for society
9.	Community is concrete	Society is abstract
10.	Community is a group of individuals	Society is a web of social relationships

3.11. Concept of Association: Association simply means a formal organisation of people. Aristotle rightly said that a man is a social animal he cannot live without society. All the basic needs of human beings are fulfilled in family. There are still many demands of needs of people which cannot be fulfilled by family or community alone. To fulfill unmet needs and demands human beings deliberately form some organisation which are called association.

3.12. Definition of Association: Association is a collection of people who come together and form some organisation to fulfill their common interests. Sociologists have defined associations differently according to MacIver, association is an organisation which is deliberately created by human beings to fulfill their interests which are common to its members. Every association has its goal and objective which it tries to achieve by different methods.

Many people in a society have some common goals and interests and they are unable to achieve them separately. To achieve these goals and fulfill common interests some people come together to form an organization and act collectively. In modern times there is large growth of associations. According to Bogardus, "association is usually a working together of people to achieve some purpose".

Association has three different meanings; i. Association is a group of people. ii. Organization is very important in this group and members of this group must have common interest or interests.

3.13. Characteristics of Association: There are various characteristics of association some of them are as follows:

i. Association is a group of people: The foundation of association is people. Every association is a group of people and there can be no association without people.

ii. Organization: Organisation is very important for every association. No association can run without organization

iii. Common interest or interests: The members of an association share common interest or interests.

iv. Membership Voluntary: The membership to an association is voluntary. An individual can become member of an association on his choice and will.

v. Size: There is no limit on the size of an association. The size of an association can be small or large

vi. Artificial: An association is formed by people for a particular interests or interests and can be disbanded after the fulfillment of that.

vii. Cooperation: Cooperation among members is very important in an association. No association can exist without the cooperation of members

viii. Rules and Regulations: There are mostly fixed and written rules which members of an association follow. The behavior of members is regulated through these rules

ix. Consciously Founded: Association is founded consciously by some people who want to achieve some common goals or interests.

x. Regulations of Relations: The relations of members are regulated through written and defined rules. A member can be expelled from an association for violating rules of association.

xi. Relations are Formal: relations in associations are formal. A member of an association has to apply for membership and may have to pay some fee.

xii. Means: Association is not an end by a means to achieve goals and fulfill interest or interests.

3.14. Differences between Society and Association: There are many differences between association and society. Following table will highlight some important difference between association and society.

S. No	Association	Society
1.	Association is artificial	Society is permanent
2.	Association is deliberately formed by man.	Society is natural
3.	Association is based on common interests	Society is based on social relations
4.	Association was formed in the later stage of human history	Society is older. It is there since man/woman is there
5.	Association is marked by cooperation	Society is marked by both cooperation and conflict
6.	Association is organized	Society may or may not be organized
7.	Membership to an association is voluntary	Membership is involuntary

3.15. Difference between Association and Community:
Association and community are two different concepts and there are various differences between them. Some of the main differences between association and community will be discussed following:

i. **Association is temporary and community is Permanent:** Association is a temporary organization of people while as community is permanent.

ii. **Common interests and we feeling:** There is common interest among the members of an association while as members of a community have we feelings and sense of belongingness.

iii. **Membership**: The membership to a community is involuntary and compulsory while as membership to an association is voluntary and optional.

iv. **Locality:** Locality is very important in community while as locality is not important for an association.

v. **Regulation of behavior**: The behavior of members in a community is regulated through customs, norms and values while as behavior of members in association is regulated by defined rules.

vi. **Organisation:** Organization is fundamental for association while as it is not important for community.

vii. Association exists within a community: Association exists within in a community. There can be many associations within a community but there can be not community within an association.

viii. A community has no legal status while as an association may have a legal status.

3.16. Long Answer Type Questions

Q. Define Society? Write down characteristics of Society?

Ans. There is no single definition of term society; different scholars have defined society differently. According to MacIver, society is a web of social relationships. The word society has been derived from the Latin word '*socius*' which means companion or associate. Society has been defined differently by various sociologists. There is not a single definition of society which is accepted by all sociologists. Sociologist is viewed as web of relationships. In this web an individual is related to other fellow being with different relations, relation of a teacher, student, buyer or seller etc. Society is not important for any particular individual but mandatory for every human. Men and women cannot live without society. Society is very fundamental for human beings. Human beings are just biological beings when they are born. They are made social beings by society.

Characteristics of society: There are various features of a society; some of them are as follows:

i. Collection of Humans: The first and the foremost important feature of society is that it is collection of individuals. As there can be no life without water and oxygen on the earth similarly there can no society without humans on the earth.

ii. Interdependence: Human beings are interdependent on each other for sustenance. Interdependence is another important feature of human society.

iii. Interaction: Whatever may be the type of a society-simple or complex, members of a society continuously interact with each other.

iv. Mutual Awareness: The mere collection of individuals does not constitute society. The members of society must be mutually aware of their relationship; the behavior of one person influences the behavior of other. According to Bhushan and Sachdeva, the journey of two persons in a train in a same compartment does not make them society. But their mutual awareness make the so.

v. Likeness: One of the important features of all societies is likeness. No matter whether it is rural or urban society, modern or traditional society likeness among members is very essential. According to MacIver "society means likeness". People in society have likeness with respect to their daily, needs, norms and values.

vii. Differences: In addition to likeness, difference is another essential feature of a society. Differences are not found only in modern societies but in simple and tribal societies also. I simple and tribal society people have differences based on age and sex and in modern societies it is based on wealth, power, occupation and education.

viii. Cooperation: Cooperation is one of the most important features of a society. Cooperation is the fundamental feature needed by a society; a society cannot exist without cooperation.

ix. Division of labour: Division of labour in society means assignment different jobs to different members of society. The assignment of these jobs is decided by culture, norm and values of society. The cooperation in a society is mostly possible with the division of labour. The division of labour in society keeps members interdependent.

x. Social Control: Social control is one of the important features of a society. To check the behavior of members and make them to follow norms and values of society social control is used. The behavior of members of society is regulated through social control. It protects from becoming deviant or rebellious. Social control is also used to suppress rebellion, revolt and conflict in society.

xi. Dynamic: Change is the law of Nature. Society is dynamic, no society ever remains same, and every society changes with changing times. Old members of a society die and new ones are born. There is change in social institution and norms of a society.

Q. Write a detailed note on community. Discuss various features of Community.

Ans. The word community has been derived from old French word *comunete* means commonness or everybody. The word has also its origin in Latin word *communis* meaning common or fellowship.

Community is an organisation of human beings who have some sense of we-feeling and belongingness. Community is a group of people living in a definite area or territory and has common sentiments or feelings.

According to MacIver, locality and community sentiments are the bases of community.

 Community is a group of people having locality and we-feeling. Following are the main characteristics of community.

i. Group of People: The very foundation of community is human beings. There certain species who live in society and communities but sociology is not concerned with them sociology is concerned with human community.

ii. Locality: Locality means that people live together in a particular geographical area. Locality gives strong social bond between members of society. The physical boundaries of a community are clearly demarcated. The members of a community make change their locality from time to time as done by tribes and nomads.

iii. Close social relations: When people live in a definite territory they develop close relation with each other. In a community members have close relation with each other.

iv. We-feeling: People living in a community have always feeling of belongingness. The members have common interests and we feeling.

v. Cultural Similarity: the members of a community have mostly common belief system, norms and values. Their food habits and other activities are almost similar. They have culture similarity.

vi. Natural: Communities are not formed by individuals on their choice but are natural. An individual is not born in a community according to his/her wish.

vii Permanent: Community is not something which can be abolished. Community is permanent.

viii. Likeness: Likeness dominates a community. The members of a community are like in respect of language, customs, and norm.

ix. Particular Name: Every community is known by a particular name.

x. Membership is involuntary: The membership to a community is involuntary. An individual is not born in a community on his/her choice.

xi. No Legal Status: a community has any legal status.

Q. Write a detailed note on Association and its features.

Ans. Association simply means a formal organisation of people. Aristotle rightly said that a man is a social animal he cannot live without society. All the basic needs of human beings are fulfilled in family. There are still many demands of needs of people which cannot be fulfilled by family or community alone. To fulfill unmet needs and demands human beings deliberately form some organisation which are called association.

Association is a collection of people who come together and form some organisation to fulfill their common interests. Sociologists have defined associations differently according to MacIver, association is an organisation which is deliberately created by human beings to fulfill their interests which are common to its members. Every association has its goal and objective which it tries to achieve by different methods.

Many people in a society have some common goals and interests and they are unable to achieve them separately. To achieve these goals and fulfill common interests some people come together to form an organization and act collectively. In modern times there is large growth of associations. According to Bogardus, "association is usually a working together of people to achieve some purpose".

Association has three different meanings; i. Association is a group of people. ii. Organization is very important in this group and members of this group must have common interest or interests.

Characteristics of Association: There are various characteristics of association some of them are as follows:

i. Association is a group of people: The foundation of association is people. Every association is a group of people and there can be no association without people.

ii. Organization: Organisation is very important for every association. No association can run without organization.

iii. Common interest or interests: The members of an association share common interest or interests.

iv. Membership Voluntary: The membership to an association is voluntary. An individual can become member of an association on his choice and will.

v.Size: There is no limit on the size of an association. The size of an association can be small or large vi.Artificial: An association is formed by people for a particular interests or interests and can be disbanded after the fulfillment of that.

vii.Cooperation: Cooperation among members is very important in an association. No association can exist without the cooperation of members

viii.Rules and Regulations: There are mostly fixed and written rules which members of an association follow. The behavior of members is regulated through these rules

ix.Consciously Founded: Association is founded consciously by some people who want to achieve some common goals or interests.

x.Regulations of Relations: The relations of members are regulated through written and defined rules. A member can be expelled from an association for violating rules of association.

xi.Relations are Formal: relations in associations are formal. A member of an association has to apply for membership and may have to pay some fee.

xii.Means: Association is not an end by a means to achieve goals and fulfill interest or interests.

3.16. Short Answer Type Questions

Q.What is main differences between Association and Community?

Or

Highlight various differences between Community and Association.

Ans. Association and community are two different concepts and there are various differences between them. Some of the main differences between association and community will be discussed following:

i. Association is temporary and community is Permanent: Association is a temporary organization of people while as community is permanent.

ii. Common interests and we feeling: There is common interest among the members of an association while as members of a community have we feelings and sense of belongingness.

iii. Membership: The membership to a community is involuntary and compulsory while as membership to an association is voluntary and optional.

iv. Locality: Locality is very important in community while as locality is not important for an association.

v. Regulation of behavior: The behavior of members in a community is regulated through customs, norms and values while as behavior of members in association is regulated by defined rules.

vi. Organisation: Organization is fundamental for association while as it is not important for community.

vii. Association exists within a community: Association exists within in a community. There can be many associations within a community but there can be not community within an association.

Q. Discuss various differences between Society and Association.

 Ans. There are many differences between association and society. Following are some important difference between association and society.

1. Association is artificial while as Society is permanent

2. Association is deliberately formed by man while as society is natural

3. Association is based on common interests while as society is based on social relations

4. Association was formed in the later stage of human history while as society is older. It is there since man/woman is there

5. Association is marked by cooperation while as society is marked by both cooperation and conflict

6. Association is organized while as society may or may not be organized

7. Membership to an association is voluntary while as Membership is involuntary to society

Q. Write a short note on Association.

Ans. Association is a collection of people who come together and form some organisation to fulfill their common interests. Sociologists have defined associations differently according to MacIver, association is an organisation which is deliberately created by human beings to fulfill their interests which are common to its members. Every association has its goal and objective which it tries to achieve by different methods.

Many people in a society have some common goals and interests and they are unable to achieve them separately. To achieve these goals and fulfill common interests some people come together to form an organization and act collectively. In modern times there is large growth of associations. According to Bogardus, "association is usually a working together of people to achieve some purpose".

Association has three different meanings; i. Association is a group of people. ii. Organization is very important in this group and members of this group must have common interest or interests.

Chapter- IV. Basic Concepts –II

4.01. Introduction: Aristotle rightly remarked that man is a social animal. He/she cannot live without society. It has been found that it is in the nature of human beings that they like to have a company of other fellow beings. Under normal circumstances human beings prefer the company of other human beings. Since times immemorial human beings have preferred company of other fellow beings. This company of human beings is known as social group.

In a society human beings have different interaction with different fellow beings. The difference is social interaction leads different kinds of relations with different fellow beings or groups. The relation with family is different from relation with neighbors. Human beings create different kinds of groups. Sociologists have differentiated these groups into many types by using many parameters.

4.02. Defining a social group: An individual does not live alone in society. He or she live together with other human beings and like to have a group life. A social group is different from society. Social group consist several individuals which exist in a society.

Social group is fundamental for existence of society. There cannot be any society without out a social group. The concept of social group is very important in sociology. Sociologists have classified social groups into different types and have given different definitions of social groups. MacIver and Page , defined social group as " any collection of human beings who are brought into human relationships with one another". Bogardus said "a social group may be thought of as a number of persons, two or more, who have some common objects of attention, who are stimulating to each other, who have common loyalty, and participate in similar activities".

4.03. Importance of Social Groups: It is not possible for an individual to live his or her life alone. It is neither possible nor feasible for a normal human being to live in isolation. He is depends on other human beings for biological, social, economic and political needs. He also requires emotional support from others. This all needs are fulfilled in a social group. We cannot even think of society without a social group. If society is a body human beings are cells and groups are tissues. As it is impossible to have a tissue without a cell it is impossible to have body without tissue. As long as human beings and society is there, there will be social groups. Social groups make life of human beings possible.

4.04. Characteristics of Social groups: Social are part and parcel of human society. They have different characteristics; some of them are briefly discussed as follows:

i. Collection of individuals: No matter what is name and nature of a social group it is collection of human beings. Social groups are formed by humans.

ii. Reciprocal Relations: In every social group there are reciprocal relations between the members of a group. Reciprocal relationship is important feature of a social group.

iii. Group Norms: Every social group has its own norms and regulations.

iv. Sense of Unity: The members of a social group have sense of unity. They are united with each other by the sense of unity. By sense of unity members follow group norms and remain loyal to their group.

v. Common Interests: The members of a social group share common interests. Common interests among the members of a group keep them united.

vi. Similar Behavior: The members of a social group behave similarly. By having similar behavior they achieve or work for common goals.

vii. Awareness: The members of a social group know that they belong to the group.

4.05: Difference between Group and Society: There are various differences between a social group and society. Some of the main differences between social group and society are briefly discussed as follows:

A social group is collection of individuals while as society is web of social relationships.

A social group is created artificially while as society is created naturally.

A social group exists within a society while society does not exist within a social group.

The membership to a social group is voluntary while as membership to society is involuntary.

A social group is always organized while as society may be unorganized.

A social group is created for a specific purpose but society is for a general purpose.

A social group may be temporary while as society is permanent.

4.06: Difference between a Social Group and Community: There are many differences between a social group and community. Following are main difference between the two.

A social group is formed with a certain purposes but a community is a natural entity.

A social group is artificial while as community is permanent.

The membership to a social group is voluntary while as membership to a community is involuntary.

A social group is part of a community while as community is a whole.

4.07. Classification of Groups: Sociologists have divided social groups into various types. Some of the important types are: Primary group, secondary group, Reference group, in group, and out group.

4.08. Primary Group: The concept of Primary group has been introduced by C. H Cooley. According to him primary group is a group of people characterized by intimate face to face association and cooperation.

The size of a primary group is small. Its members have face to face interaction. According to Cooley the social nature of an individual is framed by primary group. The relations of members in primary group are close with each other. The members of a primary group have we feelings. Primary group has profound influence on an individual. Family is an example of a primary group.

4.09. Characteristics of a Primary Group: The main characteristics of primary group are: intimate relations, physical nearness, small size face to face interaction, stability, limited self interest, similar background, and personal relations.

i. Intimate Relations: The members of a primary group have intimate relationship with each other.

ii. Physical Nearness: People in a primary group live together. Whether it is a family or neighborhood people live together. They enjoy, suffer, celebrate and mourn together.

iii. Small Size: The size of a primary group is always small and limited.

iv. Face to Face Interaction: One of the main feature of a primary group is face to face interaction. The members of a primary group have face to face interaction with each other.

v. Stability: Primary group is stable in comparison to other social groups.

vi. Limited Self Interest: The members of primary group have limited self interests. They have mostly common interests. They come together and cooperate with each other with common interests.

vii. Similar Background: The members of a primary group are not close to each other in physically but socially also. The members of family have blood or social relations with each other and neighbors have also close relations with each other.

viii. Personal Relationship: The relations in primary group are personal. The members know each other and have personal interaction. The relations are respected by the members of a primary group.

ix. Membership involuntary: The membership to a primary group is involuntary. An individual cannot join a primary group on his own will.

4.10. Importance of Primary Group: Every social institutions and group plays it function and has its own importance in society. As different organs of a human body play their role for the function of the whole body, similarly social groups play its role for the function of society. Primary group is one of the important organs of society and plays an important role in the function of society. As heart is important for the life of human being similarly primary group is important for society. Some of the main functions played by primary group are as follows:

i. Primary group adds new members to society.

ii. The basic needs of human beings are fulfilled in family.

iii. Primary group socialize new members of society. It is in the primary group where new members learn how to behave with other.

iv. The norms, values and culture of society are learned in primary group.

v. Primary group fulfills social, emotional and biological needs of members.

4.11. Secondary Group: All other groups other than primary group are called secondary groups. According to Davis secondary group is opposite to primary group.

Secondary groups are considered less important than primary group. C. H Cooly did not use the term *secondary group* but still it is attributed to him because it is understood in his "social organisation". The secondary group is that group in which face to face interaction is not important. The relations in secondary group are impersonal. It is large in size such as nation and political party. Physical nearness is not important in a secondary group.

Despite primary group and secondary group are opposite to each other both are very important and complementary to each other. An individual is members of both primary and secondary group at the same time. In modern times secondary group is also considered very important.

4.12. Characteristics of Secondary Group: Primary and secondary groups are two different social groups. The different feature of the two groups makes them different. Following are some features of secondary group.

i. Impersonal Relations: The relations in secondary group are impersonal.

ii. Large Size: The size of secondary group is large than primary group, city, town, political party, trade unions and international associations are example of secondary group.

iii. Membership Voluntary: The membership to a secondary group is voluntary. Men and women are free to join or disjoin a secondary group.

iv. Regulation of Behavior: The behavior of individuals in a secondary group is regulated through formal rules.

v. Physical Nearness: In a secondary group physical proximity is not important.

vi. Specific Interests: Secondary groups have specific interests. They are formed to fulfill common interest of members.

4. 13. Importance of Secondary groups: Both primary and secondary groups play important role and function. Despite primary group and secondary group are different from each other both are very important and complementary to each other.

Secondary groups play important role in the life of an individual especially in modern societies. Many needs of an individual which are not fulfilled in secondary group they are fulfilled through secondary group.

Secondary groups modify and reshape our attitude and behavior. In the process of socialisation secondary groups play important functions in present time. Many of the needs which are not fulfilled in a primary group are fulfilled by secondary group. The common interests of individuals who remain unmet in primary group are met in secondary group. Primary and secondary groups are complimentary to each other.

4.14. Difference between Primary and Secondary group:

There are some main differences between primary and secondary groups. Some of the main differences between the two are as under:

i. The relations in a primary group are personal while as relations in secondary group are impersonal.

ii. Face to face interaction is important in a primary group while as face to face interaction is not important in a secondary.

iii. The size of a primary group is small while as size of a secondary group is large.

iv. The influence of primary group on the personality of an individual is very much while as it is limited in secondary group.

v. The primary socialisation takes place in a primary group while as secondary socialisation takes place in a secondary group.

vi. People in primary group live in a small geographic area while in secondary group people live in vast geographic area.

vii. The cooperation among the members in a primary group is direct while as cooperation in secondary group is indirect.

viii. The relations in primary group are regulated informally (norms, values and customs) while as relations in secondary group are regulated formally.

ix. The membership to a primary group is involuntary while as membership to a secondary group is voluntary.

4.15. Concept of Reference Group: Human beings imitate each other. In every society humans imitate their fellow beings as try to be and behave like them. One group becomes reference for another they want to be like them in status and position. One group becomes reference for another. Reference group is a group with which an individual identifies him or herself. The concept of reference group has been introduced by Muzafer Sheriff in Psychology and first used by Hayman in sociology (Bhushan and Sachdeva).

4.16. Defining Reference Group: According to Horton and Hunt "A reference group is any group to which we refer when we making judgments- any group whose values judgment becomes our values judgment". When an individual or group takes any decision in a particular situation by looking at the decision of other individual or group that group becomes reference group.

A group may become reference for another group in occupation, profession, religion, and politics and so on.

4.17. Characteristics of Reference Group: Following are main characteristics of a reference group.

i. A group or individual compares itself with other group.

ii. A group thinks that behavior of other group is ideal

iii. A group aspires to enjoy equal or higher status than other group.

iv. A group imitates the other group.

v. A feeling of weakness of a group. A group which imitates another group feels weakness in their position.

v. A feeling of highness in a group. A group which imitates another group feels high of another group.

4.18. Importance of Reference Group: Reference groups are important in society. Reference group keeps the spirit of struggle alive in an individual. It brings social change and mobility in society. It provides social remedies to many social problems. It creates space for accommodation, acculturation and assimilation in society.

4.19. Difference between Primary and Reference Group: The main differences between primary and reference group are as under:

i. Physical proximity is necessary in primary group while as physical proximity is not necessary.

ii. Membership to primary group is important while as there is no membership to reference group.

iii. Membership to primary group is voluntary while as there is no membership to reference group at all.

iv. In primary group relations are personal while as in reference group relations are referential.

v. Reference may be occupational while as primary group is not so.

4.20. Concept of Role and Status: The role and status are two sides of a same coin. They are supplementary and complimentary to each other. Every individual in society plays role and occupy status.

Sociologists have used the concept of role and status in two different ways. Functionalists like Merton, Parson and Linton have used them to analyse the nature of social structure. Internationalists used concept of role and status to explain the development of personality in human beings.

4.21. What is Role? The literal meaning of word role means *character* or *function*. Social role means a function expected or assigned to a person in society. In human society every person is given some job and he/she performs it. This is called role. Lundberg defined role as "a pattern of behavior expected of an individual in a certain group or situation". Role according to Kingsly Davis role is "the manner in which a person actually carries out the requirements of his position". Role is nothing but expected behavior of an individual in a society. An individual plays different role with different individuals on different positions. He/she plays a role of father or mother in family and teacher at school.

According to Linton role is dynamic or behavior part of status.

4.22 Types of Roles: Sometimes what a role individual will play is decided by custom tradition etc. Roles can be divided into many types some of the main types of roles are; prescribed role, perceived role, performed role.

Prescribed Role: Prescribed Roles are those roles which prescribes the rights and duties to a position. They are institutionalized roles.

Perceived Role: This is a role which an individual perceives he/she shall play.

Performed Role: A role person performs is called performed role. It is subject to person's personality and past experience and also called actual role.

4.23. Role Set: An individual does not play a single role in society. He plays multiple roles in society. An individual while occupying a status does not play a single role but a number of roles. A husband, for example, is also a son, neighbor, citizen etc. This is termed role set by Merton.

4.24: Characteristics of Role: Role is an expected behavior of a person in a particular status. Following are some main features of role.

i. The norms of a culture are learned through roles

ii. Role is dynamic. A person does not play a single role his/her role keeps on changing.

iii. Role training starts in early childhood.

iv. Roles are learned both consciously and unconsciously.

v. Role is behavior expected of a status.

vi. Role means set of expectations.

vii. Some roles produce personality change (Horton and Hunt,2004).

viii. Role play important role in the process of socialisation.

4.25. Status: Status is a position or rank a person holds in a group or society. Status shows who a person is. It shows whether a position of an individual is low or high in a group. The status of a person is decided by the role he/she plays in a group or society. Every society and group has its own norms and standard to evaluate a role important or unimportant and considers a status high or low accordingly. If a role is considered important in a group or society high status is ascribed to an individual and if a role is considered less important low status is given to role or individual. A person having high status in a group enjoys more respect and honor than a person who occupies low status.

According to Bukman, "status is the worth of a person as estimated by a group". Status and role are closely related with each other. They are considered two sides of a same coin. Status is a position and roles means how that position is fulfilled.

4.26. Types of Status: Ralph Linton has classified status into two types: Ascribed status and Achieved status.

Ascribed status: Ascribed status is that status which an individual receives through birth. A status ascribed by a society where efforts and qualities of an individual are not having any role is ascribed status. It is determined by sex, age, kinship, race, and social factors. It primitive societies status of a person was generally ascribed. King or Prince is an ascribed role. In monarchies a prince and does not become prince because of his efforts or quality but because he is born as prince.

Achieved Status: Achieved status is opposite of ascribed status. It is a status achieved by a person through his/ her efforts, ability, knowledge and skills. Achieved status is generally a feature of modern societies. An individual in modern society generally achieve his/her status because of his efforts and quality. An engineer doctor in society achieves his/her status. Most of the achieved statuses need formal, conscious training in formal institutions.

Achieved position is a status which is achieved by an individual by his/her choice through competition.

4.27. Explanation of Role and Status: Role and status are two important concepts in sociology. Role and status are supplementary and complimentary to each other. According to Linton role and status are two sides of a same coin. Role is behavior expected from an individual in a particular status. Statuses are occupied by individual and roles are played by them. There can be no status without a role and there cannot be any role without a status.

4.28. Values: Values literally means beliefs of a person or group in which they have an emotional attachment. Values are normally considered higher order norms. They are cultural standards which indicate the general good believed desirable in a society. Certain actions of individuals are approved or disapproved in a society through values. Values provide standards through which an individual make choices from many alternatives. Values are more concerned with what "ought" to be and less concerned with what "is". The values differ from society to society.

Through values we define and measure goodness of things in society. General guidelines are provided to individuals through values. Values refer shared standard of behavior of people in a particular group or society. Parson considered values very important for social order.

4.29. Norms: Norms are based on values and govern behavior of human beings. Norms regulate behavior of human beings in different ways. They are standard of group behavior. Norms are very important for every society and social group. No society or group can exist without norms. According to Bierstedt " a norm is a rule or standard that governors our conduct in the social situations we participate".

4.30. Characteristics of Norms: Following are the main characteristics of Norms.

i. Norms are Universal:

4.31. Function of Norms: Norms play important function and role in a society. Some of the main functions of norms are as under:

i. Norms Help in Survival: No society can exist without norms. Norms help individual to confirm to the rules of society.

ii. Guide Behavior:

iii. Maintain Social Order:

iv. Give Cohesion to society: Norms

v. Influence individual Behavior: Norms influence behavior of an individual.

4. 32. Long Answer Type Questions

Q. Define Social Group. What are main characteristics of a Social group?

Ans. An individual does not live alone in society. He or she live together with other human beings and like to have a group life. A social group is different from society. Social group consist several individuals which exist in a society.

Social group is fundamental for existence of society. There cannot be any society without out a social group. The concept of social group is very important in sociology. Sociologists have classified social groups into different types and have given different definitions of social groups. MacIver and Page , defined social group as " any collection of human beings who are brought into human relationships with one another".   Bogardus said "a social group may be thought of as a number of persons, two or more, who have some common objects of attention, who are stimulating to each other, who have common loyalty, and participate in similar activities".

It is not possible for an individual to live his or her life alone. It is neither possible nor feasible for a normal human being to live in isolation. He is depends on other human beings for biological, social, economic and political needs. He also requires emotional support from others. This all needs are fulfilled in a social group. We cannot even think of society without a social group. If society is a body human beings are cells and groups are tissues. As it is impossible to have a tissue without a cell it is impossible to have body without tissue. As long as human beings and society is there, there will be social groups. Social groups make life of human beings possible.

Characteristics of Social groups: Social are part and parcel of human society. They have different characteristics; some of them are briefly discussed as follows:

i. Collection of individuals: No matter what is name and nature of a social group it is collection of human beings. Social groups are formed by humans.

ii. Reciprocal Relations: In every social group there are reciprocal relations between the members of a group. Reciprocal relationship is important feature of a social group.

iii. Group Norms: Every social group has its own norms and regulations.

iv. Sense of Unity: The members of a social group have sense of unity. They are united with each other by the sense of unity. By sense of unity members follow group norms and remain loyal to their group.

v. Common Interests: The members of a social group share common interests. Common interests among the members of a group keep them united.

vi. Similar Behavior: The members of a social group behave similarly. By having similar behavior they achieve or work for common goals.

vii. Awareness: The members of a social group know that they belong to the group.

Q. Status and Role are two sides of a same coin Discuss

Ans. The role and status are two sides of a same coin. They are supplementary and complimentary to each other. Every individual in society plays role and occupy status.

Sociologists have used the concept of role and status in two different ways. Functionalists like Merton, Parson and Linton have used them to analyse the nature of social structure. Internationalists used concept of role and status to explain the development of personality in human beings.

The literal meaning of word role means *character* or *function*. Social role means a function expected or assigned to a person in society. In human society every person is given some job and he/she performs it. This is called role. Lundberg defined role as "a pattern of behavior expected of an individual in a certain group or situation". Role according to Kingsly Davis role is "the manner in which a person actually carries out the requirements of his position". Role is nothing but expected behavior of an individual in a society. An individual plays different role with different individuals on different positions. He/she plays a role of father or mother in family and teacher at school.

According to Linton role is dynamic or behavior part of status.

Role is an expected behavior of a person in a particular status.

i. The norms of a culture are learned through roles

ii. Role is dynamic. A person does not play a single role his/her role keeps on changing.

iii. Role training starts in early childhood.

iv. Roles are learned both consciously and unconsciously.

v. Role is behavior expected of a status.

vi. Role means set of expectations.

vii. Some roles produce personality change (Horton and Hunt,2004).

viii. Role play important role in the process of socialisation.

Status is a position or rank a person holds in a group or society. Status shows who a person is. It shows whether a position of an individual is low or high in a group. The status of a person is decided by the role he/she plays in a group or society. Every society and group has its own norms and standard to evaluate a role important or unimportant and considers a status high or low accordingly. If a role is considered important in a group or society high status is ascribed to an individual and if a role is considered less important low status is given to role or individual. A person having high status in a group enjoys more respect and honor than a person who occupies low status.

According to Bukman, "status is the worth of a person as estimated by a group". Status and role are closely related with each other. They are considered two sides of a same coin. Status is a position and roles means how that position is fulfilled.

Ralph Linton has classified status into two types: Ascribed status and Achieved status.

Ascribed status is that status which an individual receives through birth. A status ascribed by a society where efforts and qualities of an individual are not having any role is ascribed status. It is determined by sex, age, kinship, race, and social factors. It primitive societies status of a person was generally ascribed. King or Prince is an ascribed role. In monarchies a prince and does not become prince because of his efforts or quality but because he is born as prince.

Achieved status is opposite of ascribed status. It is a status achieved by a person through his/ her efforts, ability, knowledge and skills. Achieved status is generally a feature of modern societies. An individual in modern society generally achieve his/her status because of his efforts and quality. An engineer doctor in society achieves his/her status. Most of the achieved statuses need formal, conscious training in formal institutions.

4.33. Short Answer Type Questions

Q. Write a short note on Primary Group

Ans. According to C. H Cooley primary group is a group of people characterized by intimate face to face association and cooperation.

The size of a primary group is small. Its members have face to face interaction. According to Cooley the social nature of an individual is framed by primary group. The relations of members in primary group are close with each other. The members of a primary group have we feelings. Primary group has profound influence on an individual. Family is an example of a primary group.

Q. What do you mean by Reference Group?

Ans. According to Horton and Hunt "A reference group is any group to which we refer when we making judgments-any group whose values judgment becomes our values judgment". When an individual or group takes any decision in a particular situation by looking at the decision of other individual or group that group becomes reference group.

A group may become reference for another group in occupation, profession, religion, and politics and so on.

The main characteristics of a reference group are:

i. A group or individual compares itself with other group.

ii. A group thinks that behavior of other group is ideal

iii. A group aspires to enjoy equal or higher status than other group.

iv. A group imitates the other group.

v. A feeling of weakness of a group. A group which imitates another group feels weakness in their position.

v. A feeling of highness in a group. A group which imitates another group feels high of another group.

Q. Write a short note on value and norms.

Ans. Values literally means beliefs of a person or group in which they have an emotional attachment. Values are normally considered higher order norms. They are cultural standards which indicate the general good believed desirable in a society. Certain actions of individuals are approved or disapproved in a society through values. Values provide standards through which an individual make choices from many alternatives. Values are more concerned with what "ought" to be and less concerned with what "is". The values differ from society to society.

Through values we define and measure goodness of things in society. General guidelines are provided to individuals through values. Values refer shared standard of behavior of people in a particular group or society. Parson considered values very important for social order.

Norms: Norms are based on values and govern behavior of human beings. Norms regulate behavior of human beings in different ways. They are standard of group behavior. Norms are very important for every society and social group. No society or group can exist without norms. According to Bierstedt " a norm is a rule or standard that governors our conduct in the social situations we participate".

Semester-II

Sociological Thought

<u>Chapter- V</u> , August Comte

Sociological Thought

5.1. Background: The growth and development of Sociology as a separate branch of science was not accidental or coincidence but emerged as science of society with the efforts of some great thinkers and scholars. Sociology emerged in Europe, with the influence and impact of social, political and economic conditions of the era. In this regard it becomes imperative to understand the social conditions and social ideas and their relationship with each other at that time. Sociologists of the time employed every effort to understand and explain the social phenomena of that time. Their thought and view point became the base for the growth and development of Sociology. It would not be wrong to say that the emergence and development of Sociology would not have been impossible without Sociological thought. However, sociologically speaking Sociological thought is itself dependable the social conditions of a particular time and place.

5.2. **Sociological Thought:** Generally speaking sociological thought is …. In brief it is nothing but nucleus of Sociology on which the very survival and development of sociology rests. According to Shankar Rao (2008), social thought gives stimulus for foundation of sociology. However, unlike social thought sociological thought is proposed in a scientific way.

Two factors influence the thinking of a man broadly divided

5.3. August Comte: A French Sociologist generally considered the Father of Sociology. He was born in France in 1798. He was a student and associate of Saint Simon.

The main contribution of August Comte is as: coined the term Sociology, Law of three stages, Positivism, statics and dynamics

Major Works of August Comte

i.   Positive Philosophy

ii.   System of Positive Polity

iii.   Religion of Humanity

5.4. Positivism: Positivism was originally the title of the positive philosophy (Mitchell,1979). The father of sociology August Comte introduced term positivism. Positivism is philosophy of science and empiricism is core of positivism. According to Collins Dictionary of Sociology positivism means " the doctrine formulated by Comte which asserts that only true knowledge , that is, knowledge which describes and explains the co-existence and succession of observable phenomenon, including both physical and social phenomenon".

Positivists believe that all knowledge is sense based. According to positivism standards of science are universal and can be applied on every field of knowledge irrespective of their subject matter.

Positivism means that methods of natural science: observation, experiment and comparison can be used in sociology to do science of society. August Comte has used positivism in two different ways: positivism as a philosophy and positivism as a method

Positivism as a Philosophy: Positivism as a philosophy believes that only valid knowledge is scientific knowledge. All knowledge according to positivism is sense based. According to August Comte no knowledge is independent of experience, perception and observation. It is possible to study social life and explain how and what makes society to function.

Superstition, myth, common sense, intuition and Metaphysics have no place in positivist philosophy. Science is model for sociology to become an independent science of society.

Positivisms as method: Besides as a philosophy August Comte used positivism as a method. Positivism as a method means that methods used by natural sciences like physics, chemistry, and astronomy etc can be used by sociology. By the methods of observation, experiment and comparison we can have positive science of society. Auguste Comte believed that like physics and other natural sciences sociology must use observation method to understand the laws governing social life.

5.5. Critical Evaluation of Positivism: Many criticisms have been leveled against positivism both as a philosophy and as a method.

Many scholars argued that positive science on the lines of society and social relations is not possible. They argue that subject matter of both natural sciences and sociology is different and methods used by natural sciences are not enough to understand society and social life.

According to Horkheimer, positivism falsely represented social action. He also criticized positivism for ignoring the role of a researcher in studying society.

Positivism has also been criticized for its failure to understand that sense experience is not enough to understand social reality. There are abstract laws and principles which are not observable.

Positivists have also been criticized for their failure to answer many questions. The failure of positivism gave birth to many new philosophies and perspective.

According to phenomenologist's positive science of society and application of scientific methods are impossible as the subject matter of natural sciences and social sciences are different.

Despite criticism and failure of positivism in answering many question positivism has a great impact of sociology presently.

5.6. Statics and Dynamics: In his book *Positive Philosophy* August Comte divided sociology into two branch static and dynamics. He was influenced by biology in dividing sociology into two branches. According to August Comte, distinction between Statics and dynamics are very important and helpful in sociology (Abraham and Morgan, 1985).

According to August Comte, Sociology is a positive science of society. It is important for sociology to discover the laws of social order and change in society. By studying social order we can understand the factors which are responsible for the existence of society. And by studying progress in society we can understand social movements in society. Statics according to August Comte means to analyse and understand structure of society. Dynamics means to study change and progress in society.

The social statics is dealing with the structure of a society. It studies social laws and rules of a society. Social dynamics studies how social changes are taking place in a society. According to Abraham and Morgan (1985) August Comte divided the concept of social statics into two parts: i. the study of the structure of human nature and ii. the study of the structure of social nature. Social dynamics means theory of progress, the

Law of Three Stages given by August Comte is an example of social dynamics as it deals with the progress and change in human society.

According to Lewis Coser, the division of sociology into statics and dynamics is very useful. Both statics and dynamics are correlated with each other. Statics helps in studying the social dynamics that is progress and evolution of society.

In sum up social statics means "the study of the laws of action reaction of the different parts of social order". Social dynamics means study of progress in human society.

5.7. Long Answer Type Questions

Q. Explain Positivism as a Doctrine and as a Method.

Or

Q. Critically Examine positivistic Philosophy

Ans. One of the main contribution of August Comte is positivism. Positivism was originally the title of the positive philosophy. The father of sociology August Comte introduced term positivism. Positivism is philosophy of science and empiricism is core of positivism. According to Collins Dictionary of Sociology positivism means " the doctrine formulated by Comte which asserts that only true knowledge , that is, knowledge which describes and explains the co-existence and succession of observable phenomenon, including both physical and social phenomenon".

Positivists believe that all knowledge is sense based. According to positivism standards of science are universal and can be applied on every field of knowledge irrespective of their subject matter.

Positivism means that methods of natural science: observation, experiment and comparison can be used in sociology to do science of society. August Comte has used positivism in two different ways: positivism as a philosophy and positivism as a method

Positivism as a Philosophy: Positivism as a philosophy believes that only valid knowledge is scientific knowledge. All knowledge according to positivism is sense based. According to August Comte no knowledge is independent of experience, perception and observation. It is possible to study social life and explain how and what makes society to function.

Superstition, myth, common sense, intuition and Metaphysics have no place in positivist philosophy. Science is model for sociology to become an independent science of society.

Positivisms as Method: Besides as a philosophy August Comte used positivism as a method. Positivism as a method means that methods used by natural sciences like physics, chemistry, and astronomy etc can be used by sociology. By the methods of observation, experiment and comparison we can have positive science of society. Auguste Comte believed that like physics and other natural sciences sociology must use observation method to understand the laws governing social life.

5.8. Critical Evaluation of Positivism: Many criticisms have been leveled against positivism both as a philosophy and as a method.

Many scholars argued that positive science on the lines of society and social relations is not possible. They argue that subject matter of both natural sciences and sociology is different and methods used by natural sciences are not enough to understand society and social life.

According to Horkheimer, positivism falsely represented social action. He also criticized positivism for ignoring the role of a researcher in studying society. Positivism has also been criticized for its failure to understand that sense experience is not enough to understand social reality. There are abstract laws and principles which are not observable.

Positivists have also been criticized for their failure to answer many questions. The failure of positivism gave birth to many new philosophies and perspective.

According to phenomenologist's positive science of society and application of scientific methods are impossible as the subject matter of natural sciences and social sciences are different.

Despite criticism and failure of positivism in answering many question positivism has a great impact of sociology presently.

5.9. Short Answer Type Questions

Q. Write a note on social Statics and Dynamics

Or

Q. What do you mean by social statics and social dynamics?

Or

Q. Briefly discuss social statics and social dynamics.

Ans. Social Statics and Dynamics are two concepts used by August Comte in dividing sociology into two. In his book *Positive Philosophy* August Comte divided sociology into two branch static and dynamics. He was influenced by biology in dividing sociology into two branches. According to August Comte, distinction between Statics and dynamics are very important and helpful in sociology.

According to August Comte, Sociology is a positive science of society. It is important for sociology to discover the laws of social order and change in society. By studying social order we can understand the factors which are responsible for the existence of society. And by studying progress in society we can understand social movements in society. Statics according to August Comte means to analyse and understand structure of society. Dynamics means to study change and progress in society.

The social statics is dealing with the structure of a society. It studies social laws and rules of a society. Social dynamics studies how social changes are taking place in a society. August Comte divided the concept of social statics into two parts: i. the study of the structure of human nature and ii. the study of the structure of social nature. Social dynamics means theory of progress, the Law of Three Stages given by August Comte is an example of social dynamics as it deals with the progress and change in human society.

According to Lewis Coser, the division of sociology into statics and dynamics is very useful. Both statics and dynamics are correlated with each other. Statics helps in studying the social dynamics that is progress and evolution of society.

In sum up social statics means "the study of the laws of action reaction of the different parts of social order". Social dynamics means study of progress in human society.

Q. What is Positivism?

Or

Q. What do you mean by positivistic philosophy?

Ans. Positivism as a philosophy which believes that only valid knowledge is scientific knowledge. All knowledge according to positivism is sense based. According to August Comte no knowledge is independent of experience, perception and observation. It is possible to study social life and explain how and what makes society to function.

Superstition, myth, common sense, intuition and Metaphysics have no place in positivist philosophy. Science is model for sociology to become an independent science of society.

Besides as a philosophy August Comte used positivism as a method. Positivism as a method means that methods used by natural sciences like physics, chemistry, and astronomy etc can be used by sociology. By the methods of observation, experiment and comparison we can have positive science of society. August Comte believed that like physics and other natural sciences sociology must use observation method to understand the laws governing social life.

Chapter- VI

Emile Durkheim

6.01. Brief Biography of Emile Durkheim: Durkheim was born in France in Epinal on 15th April 1858. Epinal was a small town in north-eastern part of France in a province that has its borders with Germany. France lost a war to Germany in 1870, and Durkheim lost his native community. This had a great influence on Durkheim.

Durkheim is first academic sociologist and first professor of sociology. Durkheim was a functionalist. His main contribution in sociology is, Division of Labour, Social Facts, Suicide, Religion- Sacred and Profane, Totem, Solidarity: Mechanical and Organic.

6.02. Major Works of Emile Durkheim

i. The Division of Labour in Society

ii. The Rules of Sociological Method

iii. Suicide

iv. The Elementary Forms of Religious Life

v. Education and Sociology

6.03. Background: Emile Durkheim put forward his theory of suicide in his book Suicide. By propounding his theory of suicide Durkheim has two objectives: to refute the then existing theories of suicide which were based on biological, psychological, climatic, geographical factors and to produce sociological explanation of suicide. Durkheim rejected every other factor other than social factors of suicide. He rejected heredity, climate, racial characteristics and imitation as cause of suicide, (Abraham and Morgan, 1985). One of the important contributions of Emile Durkheim in sociology is his theory of suicide. His book, Suicide is considered best example of connecting theory and research (Merton, 1968 quoted by Ritzer).

6. 04. Concept of Suicide: Suicide means the act of killing or ending one's own life. Suicide according Emile Durkheim is "every case of death resulting directly or indirectly from a positive or negative death performed by the victim himself and which strives to produce this result[1]". Durkheim showed that social factors are main factors responsible for the suicide of an individual. He maintained that two social facts – integration and regulation are reasons

---

[1] Cited from Sociology, Rao,p.704

for suicide (Pope, 1960, Quoted by Ritzer,2004). Integration means the strength of attachment and bond of an individual with a group or society. Regulation means the level of social constrain on individual. The suicide rate according to Durkheim goes up when the integration or regulation are too high or low, (Ritzer and Goodman, 2004) Durkheim divided suicide into various types: Egoistic, Altruistic, Anomic and Fatalistic.

6.5. Types of Suicide: Durkheim divided suicide into Egoistic, Altruistic, Anomic and Fatalistic.

i. Egoistic Suicide: Egoistic type of suicide is a type of suicide when a person gives too much importance to his or her self and his or her strength of attachment with a group or society is too weak. It is a state when an individual mainly think of his or herself. The lack of integration with a group or society is main factor for egoistic suicide. Religion and family according to Durkheim are forces of integration in society.

ii. Altruistic Suicide: Altruistic suicide is that type of suicide when an individual sacrifices his or her life for the sack of others. This type of suicide results due to too much integration of an individual with a group or society. When an individual has strong attachment or bond with a group and takes his or her life it is termed as altruistic suicide. Example of this type of suicide are practice of Sati, suicide bombing, self – immolation by Buddhist Monk and Japanese Harakiri.

iii. Anomic Suicide: This type of suicide results from normlessness or deregulation. When there is sudden change in society there is normlessness in society, suicide resulted from sudden and abrupt changes in society are termed as anomic suicide. A suicide according to Durkheim is anomic which results due to lack of regulations in society. An example of this type of suicide is when an individual suddenly loose his wealth in business and takes his life.

iv. Fatalistic Suicide: Fatalistic suicide is that type of suicide which has been less discussed by Emile Durkheim. He discussed fatalistic suicide in foot notes in his book suicide (Besnard, 1993, Quoted by Ritzer). This type of suicide is result high regulation in society or group an example of this type of suicide is suicide by a slave.

6.6. Social Fact: Social fact according to Durkheim is " every way of acting, fixed or not, capable of exercising on the individual an external constraint; or again, every way of acting which is general throughout a given society, while at the same time existing in its own right independent of its individual manifestation" Durkheim, 1982:13).

The concept of social fact is very important in sociology especially in the theory of Emile Durkheim. Durkheim defined sociology as a science of social facts. Social fact is way of acting, thinking, feeling which is general in society. Social facts according to are things which are external and coercive. Laws, customs, norms religious beliefs and language are examples of social facts.

6.7. Characteristics of Social Facts: The main characteristics of social facts are: external, constraint, independent and general.

i. External: Social facts are external. According to Durkheim social facts exist outside individual consciences.

ii. Constraint: Social facts according to Durkheim are constraint as they restrain individuals from doing certain acts. Social facts are capable of exercising external constraint upon individuals. Social facts constrain people in every walk of life. Human beings in a particular society behave in a particular way because of social facts.

iii. Independent: Social facts exist in its own right independent of its individual manifestation. They are independent of individual manifestation.

iv. General: Social facts are general throughout a given society not attached to a single individual in society.

6.8. Long Answer Type Questions

Q. Define Suicide. Explain Various Types of Suicide given by Durkheim.

Or

Critically Evaluate Durkheim's Theory of Suicide

Ans. Suicide means the act of killing or ending one's own life. Suicide according Emile Durkheim is "every case of death resulting directly or indirectly from a positive or negative death performed by the victim himself and which strives to produce this result". Durkheim showed that social factors are main factors responsible for the suicide of an individual. He maintained that two social facts – integration and regulation are reasons for suicide. Integration means the strength of attachment and bond of an individual with a group or society. Regulation means the level of social constrain on individual. The suicide rate according to Durkheim goes up when the integration or regulation are too high or low. Durkheim divided suicide into various types: Egoistic, Altruistic, Anomic and Fatalistic.

Durkheim divided suicide into Egoistic, Altruistic, Anomic and Fatalistic.

i. Egoistic Suicide: Egoistic type of suicide is a type of suicide when a person gives too much importance to his or her self and his or her strength of attachment with a group or society is too weak. It is a state when an individual mainly think of his or herself. The lack of integration with a group or society is main factor for egoistic suicide. Religion and family according to Durkheim are forces of integration in society.

ii. Altruistic Suicide: Altruistic suicide is that type of suicide when an individual sacrifices his or her life for the sack of others. This type of suicide results due to too much integration of an individual with a group or society. When an individual has strong attachment or bond with a group and takes his or her life it is termed as altruistic suicide. Example of this type of suicide are practice of Sati, suicide bombing, self – immolation by Buddhist Monk and Japanese Harakiri.

iii. Anomic Suicide: This type of suicide results from normlessness or deregulation. When there is sudden change in society there is normlessness in society, suicide resulted from sudden and abrupt changes in society are termed as anomic suicide. A suicide according to Durkheim is anomic which results due to lack of regulations in society. An example of this type of suicide is when an individual suddenly loose his wealth in business and takes his life.

v. Fatalistic Suicide: Fatalistic suicide is that type of suicide which has been less discussed by Emile Durkheim. He discussed fatalistic suicide in foot notes in his book suicide. This type of suicide is result high regulation in society or group an example of this type of suicide is suicide by a slave.

Criticism: Although Durkheim's theory of suicide is considered one of the main contributions in sociology however scholars have criticized his theory of suicide many grounds.

His theory of suicide has been criticized on the nature and validity of data employed by Emile Durkheim in analysing suicide. The theory is based upon partial statistics with small numbers.

The theory has been produced solely on secondary data which is regarded one of the shortcoming of the study.

Douglas criticized Durkheim's theory of suicide because on the classification of a death into suicide or natural death. Douglas also criticized Durkheim for defining suicide simply an acting of killing one's own self.

Atkinson criticized Durkheimian theory of suicide for using official data.

Q. Define Social Fact. What are main characteristics of Social Facts?

Ans. Social fact according to Durkheim is " every way of acting, fixed or not, capable of exercising on the individual an external constraint; or again, every way of acting which is general throughout a given society, while at the same time existing in its own right independent of its individual manifestation"

The concept of social fact is very important in sociology especially in the theory of Emile Durkheim. Durkheim defined sociology as a science of social facts. Social fact is way of acting, thinking, feeling which is general in society. Social facts according to are things which are external and coercive. Laws, customs, norms religious beliefs and language are examples of social facts.

The main characteristics of social facts are: external, constraint, independent and general.

i. External: Social facts are external. According to Durkheim social facts exist outside individual consciences.

ii. Constraint: Social facts according to Durkheim are constraint as they restrain individuals from doing certain acts. Social facts are capable of exercising external constraint upon individuals. Social facts constrain people in every walk of life. Human beings in a particular society behave in a particular way because of social facts.

iii. Independent: Social facts exist in its own right independent of its individual manifestation. They are independent of individual manifestation.

  i. General: Social facts are general throughout a given society not attached to a single individual in society.

6.09. Short Answer Type Questions

Q. Write a Short note of Suicide.

Or

Q. What is suicide?

Ans. Suicide is an act of ending one's own life. Suicide according Emile Durkheim is "every case of death resulting directly or indirectly from a positive or negative death performed by the victim himself and which strives to produce this result". Durkheim showed that social factors are main factors responsible for the suicide of an individual. He maintained that two social facts – integration and regulation are reasons for suicide Integration means the strength of attachment and bond of an individual with a group or society. Regulation means the level of social constrain on individual. The suicide rate according to Durkheim goes up when the integration or regulation are too high or low. Durkheim divided suicide into various types: Egoistic, Altruistic, Anomic and Fatalistic.

Q. Define Egoistic Suicide

Ans. Egoistic type of suicide is a type of suicide when a person gives too much importance to his or her self and his or her strength of attachment with a group or society is too weak. It is a state when an individual mainly think of his or herself. The lack of integration with a group or society is main factor for egoistic suicide. Religion and family according to Durkheim are forces of integration in society

Q. Write a short note on Altruistic Suicide

Ans. Altruistic suicide is that type of suicide when an individual sacrifices his or her life for the sack of others. This type of suicide results due to too much integration of an individual with a group or society. When an individual has strong attachment or bond with a group and takes his or her life it is termed as altruistic suicide. Example of this type of suicide are practice of Sati, suicide bombing, self – immolation by Buddhist Monk and Japanese Harakiri.

Q. What is Anomic Suicide?

Ans. Anomic suicide is result outcome of low regulation in society. This type of suicide results from normlessness or deregulation. When there is sudden change in society there is normlessness in society, suicide resulted from sudden and abrupt changes in society are termed as anomic suicide. A suicide according to Durkheim is anomic which results due to lack of regulations in society. An example of this type of suicide is when an individual suddenly loose his wealth in business and takes his life.

Chapter – VII

7.01. Brief Biography of Karl Henirich Marx: Karl Marx was a German philosopher born in 1818. He is one of the great philosophers which history has ever produced. His thought has not influenced only his contemporaries but coming generations also. He has given a new interpretation and new way to look at social reality.

The main contribution and concepts which Marx has produced in sociology is: class struggle, Historical Materialism, Dialectical materialism, Alienation, Praxis, class consciousness, surplus value, pauperization, Revolution

7.02. Major Works of Karl Marx

i.   The Economic and Philosophical Manuscript (1844)

ii.   The German Ideology (1845)

iii.   The Holy Family (1845)

iv.   The Poverty of Philosophy (1847)

v.   Wage Labour and Capital

vi.   The Communist Manifesto (1848)

vii.   Critique of Political Economy (1848)

viii.   Class Struggle in France (1850)

ix.   The Capital –I (1867)

x.   The Capital – II (1885)

7.03. Historical Materialism:

The term Historical Materialism was first used by Plekhanov by which he meant a set of assumptions, Marx used about the nature of social reality. It is the methodology used by Marx to understand social reality and its development. Marx used two opposite views on the nature of social reality: Hegalian 'Idealism' and 18th century 'Materialism' to produce his theory of historical Materialism.

Historical Materialism is also called Historical interpretation of history. Historical Materialism is one of the main contributions of Marx. Historical Materialism means throughout human history material things (matter) has profound influence on shaping progress of society. The progress and change in social, political, intellectual and relationships was shaped by matter. The economic conditions of society at a given point of time are determined by economic conditions.

Economic activity according to Marx is most important activity of mankind. The very existence of human beings is depending upon economy or material things. Historical

Materialism is regarded as general theory of Marx on society. Material conditions and factors of society affect the structure and progress. The base for change in society is material and in every period of history material condition determined change.

By his theory of Historical Materialism Marx was able to criticize capitalism.

Marx identified four stages in human history i. Primitive communism, ii. Ancient society iii. Feudal society iv. Capitalist society. Primitive communism according to him was earlier stage of society. In this stage forces of production were very simple and were owned commonly by people. In Ancient society was divided into two classes: masters and slaves. Masters were belonging to a class which owned the forces of production and slaves were owned by masters. In feudal society people were divided into two classes' landless serfs and land lords. This period was dominated by agriculture and agriculture related activities. Capitalist society emerged with the growth of industrial production and consisted two classes' bourgeoisie and proletariat. Bourgeoisie owned the forces of production and proletariat contributed by their labour. Capitalist society according to Marx is unstable and will be replaced by communist society.

Marx's showed his Historical Materialist theory by analysing of change in European society from feudalism to capitalism. Marx believed that all institutions, values, ideas and literature serve the interest of those who own the means of production.

Historical materialism is credited for playing its important role in the development of modern sociology. By the theory of Historical Materialism Marx elaborated the conception of the nature of society and introduced new elements to understand the society. Besides giving new methods of inquiry and new concepts in sociology Historical materialism also introduced critical way of thinking, (Bhowmik, et. al, 2009).

7.04. Religion Theory of Karl Marx: Karl Marx presented his views on religion in his famous book "Critique of Hegel's Philosophy of Right". He was very critic of religion and considered a tool of oppression in the hands of oppressed. According to Marx "religion is the sigh of the oppressed creature, the heart of heartless world, and the sol of soulless conditions. It is opium of the people".

Marx believed that real happiness of people lies in abolition of religion. He maintained that "the abolition of religion as the illusionary happiness of the people is the demand of their real happiness". Religion to Marx "is an illusion which eases pain produced by exploitation and oppression. It is a series of myths which justify and legitimate the subordination of the subject class and the domination and privilege of the ruling class. It is distortion of reality which provides many of the deceptions which form the basis of ruling class ideology and false class consciousness" (Harlambos 1090: 460). Religion from Marx point of view justifies social inequalities in society. The promise of rewards after death kills critical thinking in society.

According to Howard Zinn, religion has both negative and positive functions from Marxian perspective. The negative role of religion is that it is opium for masses and it plays positive functions by giving a sigh of relief to masses from the exploitation of oppressed[2].

---

[2] Howard Zinn. Howard Zinn: On Marx and Marxism" Retrieved on 10-November 2015. www.en.m.wikipedia.org/wiki/Marxism_and_religion

According to Marx, the base and foundation of most of the religions of world is in oppressed classes. The oppression they were going through provided conducive environment and fertile ground for origin of new religions. Christianity according to Engles was a movement of oppressed class, (Harlambos, 1980).

Marx believed that all institutions, values, ideas and literature serve the interest of those who own the means of production. Religious principles like Karma, justify the superior position of oppressors and keeps the oppressed lot in subjugation.

7.05. Long Answer Type Questions

Q. Explain Marx's Conception on Historical Materialism

Or

What do you mean by Materialist interpretation of History?

Ans. The term Historical Materialism was first used by Plekhanov by which he meant a set of assumptions, Marx used about the nature of social reality. It is the methodology used by Marx to understand social reality and its development. Marx used two opposite views on the nature of social reality: Hegalian 'Idealism' and 18th century 'Materialism' to produce his theory of historical Materialism.

Historical Materialism is also called Historical interpretation of history. Historical Materialism is one of the main contributions of Marx. Historical Materialism means throughout human history material things (matter) has profound influence on shaping progress of society. The progress and change in social, political, intellectual and relationships was shaped by matter. The economic conditions of society at a given point of time are determined by economic conditions.

Economic activity according to Marx is most important activity of mankind. The very existence of human beings is depending upon economy or material things. Historical Materialism is regarded as general theory of Marx on society. Material conditions and factors of society affect the structure and progress. The base for change in society is material and in every period of history material condition determined change.

By his theory of Historical Materialism Marx was able to criticize capitalism.

Marx identified four stages in human history i. Primitive communism, ii. Ancient society iii. Feudal society iv. Capitalist society. Primitive communism according to him was earlier stage of society. In this stage forces of production were very simple and were owned commonly by people. In Ancient society was divided into two classes: masters and slaves. Masters were belonging to a class which owned the forces of production and slaves were owned by masters. In feudal society people were divided into two classes' landless serfs and land lords. This period was dominated by agriculture and agriculture related activities. Capitalist society emerged with the growth of industrial production and consisted two classes' bourgeoisie and proletariat. Bourgeoisie owned the forces of production and proletariat contributed by their labour. Capitalist society according to Marx is unstable and will be replaced by communist society.

Marx's showed his Historical Materialist theory by analysing of change in European society from feudalism to capitalism. Marx believed that all institutions, values, ideas and literature serve the interest of those who own the means of production.

Historical materialism is credited for playing its important role in the development of modern sociology. By the theory of Historical Materialism Marx elaborated the conception of the nature of society and introduced new elements to understand the society. Besides giving new methods of inquiry and new concepts in sociology Historical materialism also introduced critical way of thinking.

Q. Write a detailed note on Marx's theory of Religion

Or

Religion is Opium of masses and heart of Heartless. Discuss

Ans. Karl Marx presented his views on religion in his famous book "Critique of Hegel's Philosophy of Right". He was very critic of religion and considered a tool of oppression in the hands of oppressed. According to Marx "religion is the sigh of the oppressed creature, the heart of heartless world, and the sol of soulless conditions. It is opium of the people".

Marx believed that real happiness of people lies in abolition of religion. He maintained that "the abolition of religion as the illusionary happiness of the people is the demand of their real happiness". Religion to Marx "is an illusion which eases pain produced by exploitation and oppression. It is a series of myths which justify and legitimate the subordination of the subject class and the domination and privilege of the ruling class. It is distortion of reality which provides many of the deceptions which form the basis of ruling class ideology and false class consciousness". Religion from Marx point of view justifies social inequalities in society. The promise of rewards after death kills critical thinking in society.

According to Howard Zinn, religion has both negative and positive functions from Marxian perspective. The negative role of religion is that it is opium for masses and it plays positive functions by giving a sigh of relief to masses from the exploitation of oppressed.

According to Marx, the base and foundation of most of the religions of world is in oppressed classes. The oppression they were going through provided conducive environment and fertile ground for origin of new religions. Christianity according to Engles was a movement of oppressed class.

Marx believed that all institutions, values, ideas and literature serve the interest of those who own the means of production. Religious principles like Karma, justify the superior position of oppressors and keeps the oppressed lot in subjugation.

7.06. Short Answer Type Questions

Q. Write a short note on Marx's view on Religion

Or

What is Function of Religion in Society according to Marx?

Ans. According to Marx "religion is the sigh of the oppressed creature, the heart of heartless world, and the sol of soulless conditions. It is opium of the people".

Marx believed that real happiness of people lies in abolition of religion. He maintained that "the abolition of religion as the illusionary happiness of the people is the demand of their real happiness". Religion to Marx "is an illusion which eases pain produced by exploitation and oppression. It is a series of myths which justify and legitimate the subordination of the subject class and the domination and privilege of the ruling class. It is distortion of reality which provides many of the deceptions which form the basis of ruling class ideology and false class consciousness" Religion from Marx point of view justifies social inequalities in society. The promise of rewards after death kills critical thinking in society.

Q. Write a short note on historical Materialism

Or

What is Materialistic interpretation of History?

Ans. Historical Materialism is also called Historical interpretation of history. Historical Materialism is one of the main contributions of Marx. Historical Materialism means throughout human history material things (matter) has profound influence on shaping progress of society. The progress and change in social, political, intellectual and relationships was shaped by matter. The economic conditions of society at a given point of time are determined by economic conditions.

Economic activity according to Marx is most important activity of mankind. The very existence of human beings is depending upon economy or material things. Historical Materialism is regarded as general theory of Marx on society. Material conditions and factors of society affect the structure and progress. The base for change in society is material and in every period of history material condition determined change.

By his theory of Historical Materialism Marx was able to criticize capitalism.

Chapter – IV

8.01. Brief Biography of Max Weber: Max Weber was a German sociologist. He was born in 1864.

His main contributions in society are: ideal types, interpretive sociology, social action, verstehen, bureaucracy, spirit of capitalism, authority.

8.02. Major Works of Max Weber

i.   General Economic History

ii.   The Theory of Social and Economic Organisation

iii. The City

iv.   Economy and Society

v.   The Protestant Ethics and the Spirit of Capitalism

vi.   The Methodology of Social Sciences

8.03. Social Action: Background: The concept of Social Action has significant importance in the Sociology of Max Weber. He defined sociology as "comprehensive science of social action". The subject matter of sociology according to Weber is social action. Weber said "I became one [a sociologist] in order to put an end to collectivist notions. In other words sociology too can be practiced by proceeding from the action of one or more, few or many individuals, that means, by employing a strictly 'individualist' method" (Roth, 1976: 306, Quoted by Ritzer,2004: 209).

8. 04. Meaning of Social Action: An action according to Max Weber is social action when the actor gives subjective meaning to an action of others in society. An action becomes only social action when an individual gives meaningful understanding to actions of others. An action is social action by virtue of subjective meaning attached to action or behavior of others.

8.05. Characteristics of Social Action: The main characteristics of social action are: its relation with action of others. Social action is not isolated. There are results of cooperation and struggle between individuals and social action has meaningful understanding with other actions.

i. Social Action has relation with other social actions: According to Max Weber no action becomes social action unless it has relationship with behavior of others. Others according to Weber may be known or unknown persons.

ii. Social action is not isolated: According to Weber isolated action of an actor is not social action. Action according to him becomes social action only when an actor is oriented to the behavior or action of others.

iii. Social Action is result of cooperation and struggle between individuals: The only contact of an individual with another is not always social action. In every social action there is either cooperation or conflict. When an individual is in cooperation or conflict with other individual and action with the influence of cooperation or conflict actions becomes social action. The behavior of individual may be result of friendship or enmity.

iv. Social action has meaningful understanding with other actions: When an individual gives meaningful understanding to action or behavior of others it becomes social action. Social action has always meaningful understanding with the actions of others.

8.06. Types of Social Action: Max Weber has divided social actions into four types. They are discussed briefly as follows:

i. Zweckrational Action or Rational Action: In this type of action the actor decides his goal on merit and the means are chosen on their efficiency. The efficiency of means is analysed to attain the goal. In this type of action, values, emotions and tradition has no role in selecting goal and choosing means to attain that goal.

ii. Wertrational Action or Value Oriented Action:
Wertrational action according to Max Weber is that action which actor selects his means on their efficiency and ends are determined by value. attain the goal. In this type of action the actor selects his means in terms of their efficiency to goal but ends are determined by value. In this type of action means are determined by their efficiency and goal is determined by value.

iii. Affective Action or Emotional Action: In this type of action emotions of an individual are dominant. The actor chooses his or her goal on the bases of emotions or impulses. Thus emotions and impulses determine both means and goal in affective action an example of this action is when a mother slaps her child (Abraham). Efficiency of means has no role in this type of action.

iv. Traditional Action: Traditional action according to Max Weber is that type of social action in which both means and goals are determined by custom. In this type of action the actor decides his means and goal on the influence of tradition. According to Abraham and Morgan ritual of tradition are examples of traditional action. Efficiency of means has no role to play in traditional action.

8.07. Protestant Ethic and Spirit of Capitalism: Max Weber is well known for his work 'The Protestant Ethic and the Spirit of Capitalism. Weber examined various factors responsible for the development of economy. He found positive relation between the Protestant ethics and the spirit of capitalism. He found that many Protestants own industries and posses more wealth than Catholics. Protestant ethics according to Weber is closely related with the spirit of capitalism (Abraham, 1985).

According to Abraham and Morgan, "the investigation of the relationship between religious values and economics interest was triggered by a number of factors. In the first place, Weber noticed that Protestants, particularly Protestants of certain sects, were the chief captains of industry and possessed more wealth and economic means than other religious groups, notably Catholics. Therefore, he wanted to ascertain whether there is essential harmony between the Protestant ethics and the spirit of capitalism".

Weber maintained that religious ideas of Calvinists played important role in the emergence of modern capitalism. He examined relation between capitalism and Protectionism and found many Protestants were big businessmen and industrialists. He found that modern capitalism derive its ideology that profit is an end in itself from Protestantism.

While discussing similarities between modern capitalism and Protestants Weber said that Protestants believe in predestination – that God has already decided. The status and position of a person according to Protestants has been already determined by the God. The desire of wealth is not for the enjoyment or luxurious living is philosophy of capitalism and this too has been derived from the religion. This leads desire to accumulate unlimited wealth which according to Weber is spirit of modern capitalism. Capital accumulation in many Western countries and Industrial revolution are all off shots of this belief. This not only increased production process but efficiency and discipline also.

The work is considered worship and every day is holy day. Hard work, discipline and efficiency are basis for the emergence of capitalism and this too has been derived from religion.

The main values of Protestants responsible for the emergence of Capitalism identified by Abraham and Morgan are as follows:

i. The shift from ritualistic and other worldly orientation to down –to-earth pragmatism. Protestants discouraged mysticism and encouraged this worldly asceticism and understanding of natural order. This brought discipline in the sect and favored the development of science.

ii. Changed attitude towards work: Work in Protestant doctrine a virtue, desirable and contributing to the glory of God. They encouraged not only work but hard work, efficiency and discipline.

iii. The concept of work: Calvinist sect of Protestantism believed that certain individuals are chosen by God to enter heaven and certain have to enter the hell. This is predestined. God has already determined who have to enter the Heaven and the Hell, this can't be changed by bribe or begging. Since everyone was "anxious to know if he is marked for salvation or damnation, he should select a calling, a vocation, work hard at it and be successful. The economic impact of this doctrine was profound indeed".

iv. The New attitude towards the collection of interest on loans. Protestants opposed the Catholic doctrine that collection of interest on loans is forbidden and encouraged the collection of interest on loans. This encouraged the accumulation money. This also " prompted a spurt of economic activity: establishment of lending houses, new investments and new floating capital".

v. Strictures on Alcoholism. Alcoholism and consumption of beverage is prohibited in Protestantism.

vi. Encouragement of Literacy and Learning: Protestants have strong love for literacy and learning. They consider backwardness cause of illiteracy. Every person according to their belief must be able to read Bible on his or her own so that he or she can understand Bible on his/ her own. This will save a person from priestly interpretation of Bible. This belief according to Weber became base for modern education and modern education and capitalism are correlated with each other.

vii. Rejection of Holidays: For Protestants every holy day is holy day with work. A day is holy day for an individual on which he or she works. They rejected Catholic calendar which was full of holidays. This led factories and offices to work seven days in a week leading more capital accumulation.

viii. Protestant Asceticism: Protestants believe that one should not indulge in this earthy thing as they lead to sins and disorder and therefore a person should keep his or her self away from pleasure of this world. This led the accumulation of money and forbids money to be used for pleasure.

8.08. Long Answer Type Question

Q. What is Social action? What are different types of social action according to Weber?

Or

Q. Discuss social action. What is typology of social action?

An action according to Max Weber is social action when the actor gives subjective meaning to an action of others in society. An action becomes only social action when an individual gives meaningful understanding to actions of others. An action is social action by virtue of subjective meaning attached to action or behavior of others.

i. Zweckrational Action or Rational Action: In this type of action the actor decides his goal on merit and the means are chosen on their efficiency. The efficiency of means is analysed to attain the goal. In this type of action, values, emotions and tradition has no role in selecting goal and choosing means to attain that goal.

ii. Wertrational Action or Value Oriented Action: Wertrational action according to Max Weber is that action which actor selects his means on their efficiency and ends are determined by value. attain the goal. In this type of action the actor selects his means in terms of their efficiency to goal but ends are determined by value. In this type of action means are determined by their efficiency and goal is determined by value.

iii. Affective Action or Emotional Action: In this type of action emotions of an individual are dominant. The actor chooses his or her goal on the bases of emotions or impulses. Thus emotions and impulses determine both means and goal in affective action an example of this action is when a mother slaps her child (Abraham). Efficiency of means has no role in this type of action.

v. Traditional Action: Traditional action according to Max Weber is that type of social action in which both means and goals are determined by custom. In this type of action the actor decides his means and goal on the influence of tradition. According to Abraham and Morgan ritual of tradition are examples of traditional action. Efficiency of means has no role to play in traditional action.

Q. Write a detailed note on "The Protestant Ethic and the Spirit of Capitalism.

Or

Q. What is relation between Religion and Capitalism? Discuss from Webrian Perspective.

Or

Q. What were the main values of Protestantism responsible for the development of capitalism?

Or

Q. Critically Evaluate Weber's theory of Capitalism and Religion

Ans. 'The Protestant Ethic and the Spirit of Capitalism' is one of the notable contributions of Max Weber. In this classical work Weber examined various factors responsible for the development of economy. He found positive relation between the Protestant ethics and the spirit of capitalism. He found that many Protestants own industries and posses more wealth than Catholics. Protestant ethics according to Weber is closely related with the spirit of capitalism.

Weber maintained that religious ideas of Calvinists played important role in the emergence of modern capitalism. He examined relation between capitalism and Protectionism and found many Protestants were big businessmen and industrialists. He found that modern capitalism derive its ideology that profit is an end in itself from Protestantism.

While discussing similarities between modern capitalism and Protestants Weber said that Protestants believe in predestination – that God has already decided. The status and position of a person according to Protestants has been already determined by the God. The desire of wealth is not for the enjoyment or luxurious living is philosophy of capitalism and this too has been derived from the religion. This leads desire to accumulate unlimited wealth which according to Weber is spirit of modern capitalism. Capital accumulation in many Western countries and Industrial revolution are all off shots of this belief. This not only increased production process but efficiency and discipline also.

The work is considered worship and every day is holy day. Hard work, discipline and efficiency are basis for the emergence of capitalism and this too has been derived from religion.

The main values of Protestants responsible for the emergence of Capitalism identified by Abraham and Morgan are as follows:

i. The shift from ritualistic and other worldly orientation to down –to-earth pragmatism.   Protestants discouraged mysticism and encouraged this worldly asceticism and understanding of natural order. This brought discipline in the sect and favored the development of science.

ii. Changed attitude towards work: Work in Protestant doctrine a virtue, desirable and contributing to the glory of God. They encouraged not only work but hard work, efficiency and discipline.

iii. The concept of work: Calvinist sect of Protestantism believed that certain individuals are chosen by God to enter heaven and certain have to enter the hell. This is predestined. God has already determined who have to enter the Heaven and the Hell; this can't be changed by bribe or begging. Since everyone was "anxious to know if he is marked for salvation or damnation, he should select a calling, a vocation, work hard at it and be successful. The economic impact of this doctrine was profound indeed".

iv. The New attitude towards the collection of interest on loans. Protestants opposed the Catholic doctrine that collection of interest on loans is forbidden and encouraged the collection of interest on loans. This encouraged the accumulation money. This also "prompted a spurt of economic activity: establishment of lending houses, new investments and new floating capital".

v. Strictures on Alcoholism. Alcoholism and consumption of beverage is prohibited in Protestantism.

vi. Encouragement of Literacy and Learning: Protestants have strong love for literacy and learning. They consider backwardness cause of illiteracy. Every person according to their belief must be able to read Bible on his or her own so that he or she can understand Bible on his/ her own. This will save a person from priestly interpretation of Bible. This belief according to Weber became base for modern education and modern education and capitalism are correlated with each other.

vii. Rejection of Holidays: For Protestants every holy day is holy day with work. A day is holy day for an individual on which he or she works. They rejected Catholic calendar which was full of holidays. This led factories and offices to work seven days in a week leading more capital accumulation.

viii. Protestant Asceticism: Protestants believe that one should not indulge in this earthy thing as they lead to sins and disorder and therefore a person should keep his or her self away from pleasure of this world. This led the accumulation of money and forbids money to be used for pleasure.

Criticism: Weber has been criticized for his theory of capitalism and religion. Weber has been criticized for the assumption that capitalism is growth of Protestant ethics. The capitalism was a growing face before that reformation in Christianity which gave birth to Protestants. Another point against his theory is that asceticism was not a factor for the emergence of capitalism but logic and rationality.

According to Amintore, capitalism in Europe has developed before protestant revolt so it is irrational to link capitalism with Protestants.

According to Tawney, that there is no relation between capitalism and Protestants, he said that there is negative relation between the two.

8.09. Short Answer Type Questions

Q. What is social action? Discuss main Characteristics of a social action.

Ans. An action according to Max Weber is social action when the actor gives subjective meaning to an action of others in society. An action becomes only social action when an individual gives meaningful understanding to actions of others. An action is social action by virtue of subjective meaning attached to action or behavior of others.

The main characteristics of social action are: its relation with action of others. Social action is not isolated. There are results of cooperation and struggle between individuals and social action has meaningful understanding with other actions.

i. Social Action has relation with other social actions: According to Max Weber no action becomes social action unless it has relationship with behavior of others. Others according to Weber may be known or unknown persons.

ii. Social action is not isolated: According to Weber isolated action of an actor is not social action. Action according to him becomes social action only when an actor is oriented to the behavior or action of others.

iii. Social Action is result of cooperation and struggle between individuals: The only contact of an individual with another is not always social action. In every social action there is either cooperation or conflict. When an individual is in cooperation or conflict with other individual and action with the influence of cooperation or conflict actions becomes social action. The behavior of individual may be result of friendship or enmity.

iv. Social action has meaningful understanding with other actions: When an individual gives meaningful understanding to action or behavior of others it becomes social action. Social action has always meaningful understanding with the actions of others.

Max Weber has divided social actions into four types. They are discussed briefly as follows:

Q. Write a short note on social action

Or

Q. Action and social action are two different concepts. Discuss.

Ans. The concept of Social Action has significant importance in the Sociology of Max Weber. He defined sociology as "comprehensive science of social action". The subject matter of sociology according to Weber is social action.

An action according to Max Weber is social action when the actor gives subjective meaning to an action of others in society. An action becomes only social action when an individual gives meaningful understanding to actions of others. An action is social action by virtue of subjective meaning attached to action or behavior of others.

Q. What were the main values of Protestants according to Weber responsible for the development of Capitalism?

Ans. The main values of Protestants responsible for the emergence of Capitalism identified by Abraham and Morgan are as follows:

i. The shift from ritualistic and other worldly orientation to down –to-earth pragmatism. Protestants discouraged mysticism and encouraged this worldly asceticism and understanding of natural order. This brought discipline in the sect and favored the development of science.

ii. Changed attitude towards work: Work in Protestant doctrine a virtue, desirable and contributing to the glory of God. They encouraged not only work but hard work, efficiency and discipline.

iii. The concept of work: Calvinist sect of Protestantism believed that certain individuals are chosen by God to enter heaven and certain have to enter the hell. This is predestined. God has already determined who have to enter the Heaven and the Hell; this can't be changed by bribe or begging. Since everyone was "anxious to know if he is marked for salvation or damnation, he should select a calling, a vocation, work hard at it and be successful. The economic impact of this doctrine was profound indeed".

iv. The New attitude towards the collection of interest on loans. Protestants opposed the Catholic doctrine that collection of interest on loans is forbidden and encouraged the collection of interest on loans. This encouraged the accumulation money. This also "prompted a spurt of economic activity: establishment of lending houses, new investments and new floating capital".

v. Strictures on Alcoholism. Alcoholism and consumption of beverage is prohibited in Protestantism.

vi. Encouragement of Literacy and Learning: Protestants have strong love for literacy and learning. They consider backwardness cause of illiteracy. Every person according to their belief must be able to read Bible on his or her own so that he or she can understand Bible on his/ her own. This will save a person from priestly interpretation of Bible. This belief according to Weber became base for modern education and modern education and capitalism are correlated with each other.

vii. Rejection of Holidays: For Protestants every holy day is holy day with work. A day is holy day for an individual on which he or she works. They rejected Catholic calendar which was full of holidays. This led factories and offices to work seven days in a week leading more capital accumulation.

viii. Protestant Asceticism: Protestants believe that one should not indulge in this earthy thing as they lead to sins and disorder and therefore a person should keep his or her self away from pleasure of this world. This led the accumulation of money and forbids money to be used for pleasure.

Bibliography

Abercrombie, Nicholas. et.al (1984). Dictionary of Sociology. England. Penguine Books.

Abraham, Francis and Morgan, John. Henry. (1985). Sociological Thought. New Delhi. Trinity

Aron, Raymond (1967). Main Currents in Sociological Thought. Middlessex. Penguin

Atal, Yogesh. (2012) Sociology: A Study of Social Sphere. India. Dorling Kindrsley Pvt. Ltd

Bhowmik, et. al, (2009). Sociological Thought New Delhi. IGNOU

Bottomore, T. B. (1972) Sociology: A guide to problems and Literature. New Delhi Blackie and Son (India) LTD

Bierstedt, Robert, (1963). The Social order: an introduction to Sociology. McGraw-Hill

Bhushan, Vidya and Sachdeva, D. R (1961).(Reprint 2013). An Introduction to Sociology. Allahabad. Kitab Mahal

Bhushan, Vidya and Sachdeva, D. R (2012). Fundamentals of Sociology. New Delhi. Pearson

Blumer, Herbert and Shibutani Tamotsu.(eds).(1970)Human Nature and collective Behaviour: Papers in Herbert Blumer. USA. Prentice Hall

Gauba, O.P. (2007). Political Theory and Thought. Noida. Maysoor Paperbacks

Gauba, O.P. (2009). An Introduction to Political Theory. Delhi. Macmillan

Horton, Paul.B. and Hunt, Chester. L (2004). Sociology. New Delhi. Tata McGraw-Hill

Haralambos, M and Heald, R. M. (1980). Sociology: Themes and Perspectives. New Delhi. Oxford University Press.

Husain, S. (2007). Sociology. New Delhi. True Book Company

Inkles, Alex (1987). What is Sociology? New Delhi. Prentice Hall of India.

Johson. Harry. M. (1995). Sociology A Systematic Introduction. New Delhi.

Kachroo,J.L and Kachroo Vijay (1981). General Sociology. New Delhi. Cosmos Bookhive

Kar, Primal.B (NA) Society: A study of Social Interaction.. New Delhi. Jawhar Publishers

MacIver, R. M. and Page, C.H (2007). Society introductory Analysis. New Delhi. Macmillan India Ltd.

Mitchell, G. Duncan. (1975). Dictionary of Sociology. Rutledge

NCERT. (2006). Introducing Sociology. New Delhi. NCERT

Nisbet, Robert. A . (1943). The French Revolution and the Rise of Sociology in France. *American Journal of Sociology* . Vol. 49, No.2, pp.156-164

Ogburn, William.F and Nimkoff, M.F. (2011). Sociology .New Delhi. Saup Book Publishers

Oommen, T.K, and Venugopal. (1988). Sociology: For Law Student. Lucknow. Eastern Book Company.

Rao , C.N. Shankar. (1990). Sociology: Principles of sociology with an introduction to Social Thought. New Delhi. S. Chand.

Ritzer, George and Goodman, Douglas.J. (2004). Classical Sociological Theory. New York. McGraw Hill

Singh, Yogendra. (2009). Sociological Thought. New Delhi. IGNOU

www.ingramcontent.com/pod-product-compliance
Lightning Source LLC
Chambersburg PA
CBHW071351280526
45787CB00001B/288